Workplace S

Related titles by Law Society Publishing

Employment Law Handbook
Daniel Barnett and Henry Scrope
1 85328 716 4

Equal Pay
Sara Leslie, Sue Hastings and Jo Morris
1 85328 827 6

TUPE
Gill Sage
1 85328 815 2

Wrongful Dismissal
Julian Yew
1 85328 762 8

Titles from Law Society Publishing can be ordered from all good bookshops or direct from our distributors, Marston Book Services (tel. 01235 465656 or email law.society@marston.co.uk). For further information or a catalogue call our editorial and marketing office on 020 7320 5878.

WORKPLACE STRESS

Law and Practice

Smita Jamdar and Jane Byford

The Law Society

ISBN 1–85328–837–3

Published in 2003 by the Law Society
113 Chancery Lane, London WC2A 1PL

Crown copyright material is reproduced with the permission of the Controller of Her Majesty's Stationery Office

Typeset by J&L Composition, Filey, North Yorkshire
Printed by Antony Rowe Ltd, Chippenham, Wilts

Contents

Preface

Workplace stress can be a legal and managerial minefield and with stress claims of all types seemingly on the increase, it is now more important than ever for employers to manage stress-related illnesses appropriately, fairly and consistently in order to avoid liability.

The first problem is usually one of definition: what is workplace stress? Stress can manifest itself in many different ways, be they physical, psychological or behavioural. It can also be difficult to identify the causes of stress and to take steps to prevent it arising, because what causes one person to suffer from a stress-related illness can be the source of another person's adrenalin rush.

One of the other major difficulties for employees, employers and those advising them is that stress can give rise to a variety of different legal liabilities, crossing a number of legal disciplines. Smita Jamdar, as a litigator, is most likely to come across stress in the context of a personal injury claim or in a health and safety context. On the other hand, as an employment lawyer, I am most likely to see the issue of stress arising in the context of a sexual harassment, disability discrimination or constructive dismissal claim. However, it can be a mistake to pigeonhole stress claims rather than looking at the issue in a wider context.

Since the Court of Appeal's decision in *Hatton v. Sutherland* last year, it has become more difficult for employees to bring successful stress-related personal injury claims, but this has only meant that employees have had to be more inventive and think more laterally about the types of claims they can bring. The importance of looking at stress in the context of all the relevant legislation cannot be over-emphasised.

In writing this book Smita and I have tried to draw together all the strands of possible legal liability and approach workplace stress and the claims that can arise from it in a practical way, rather than considering it in the context of one type of liability alone. We have also attempted to provide some guidance on how to proactively manage workplace stress rather than taking a reactive approach once a claim has been received. Although it will never be possible to eliminate stress in the workplace completely, adopting good management practice can help minimise the risk of claims arising in the first place and put an employer in a better position to defend a claim if it does arise.

The law is stated as at 31 July 2003.

Jane Byford
August 2003

Table of cases

Table of statutes

Table of statutory instruments and European legislation

CHAPTER 1

Defining the problem

1.1 INTRODUCTION

Workplace stress is widely considered to be one of the key occupational health issues of modern times and has been described as 'the most dangerous emerging risk to business in the early part of the 21st century' (Association of Insurers and Risk Managers). It poses a number of challenges to businesses: operational (in the form of absenteeism and poor productivity); managerial (interpersonal problems and conflicts often arise); and legal (claims for compensation can be brought on a number of different grounds, in a number of different forms and can be uninsured).

Individuals affected by stress-related illnesses may pay a high cost in terms of the damage to their lives, their relationships and their futures. It is difficult to find reliable statistics of the scale of the problem, but the general perception seems to be that damaging levels of workplace stress are on the increase in most business sectors and that this is bad for business and bad for the individuals involved.

This chapter aims to provide an overview of the nature and extent of the problem and to explore some of the reasons why the legal position, in terms of employers' duties to address the undoubtedly widespread problem, is so complex.

1.2 WHAT IS STRESS?

There is, unfortunately, no agreed definition of 'stress'. From a practical viewpoint, some of the best definitions are those which reflect the fact that, ultimately, every individual will have their own perception of what constitutes stress, such as:

> Any factor or event(s) that threaten a person's health or adversely affects his or her normal functioning. (*Black's Medical Dictionary*)

or

> A vague catch all, used by different people to mean different things. It is used to describe both physical and mental conditions, and the pressures which cause those conditions. It is also used to describe stress which is beneficial and harmful both in its forces and its effects. *(Addressing the Public Sector – Nurses, Police, Social Workers and Teachers (1998))*

Although these definitions may most accurately reflect the reality of the situation, they are too broad in scope and too uncertain to use as a basis for consideration of legal duties or liabilities. One of the most widely accepted definitions of stress in case authorities is:

> The reaction people have to excessive pressures or other types of demand placed upon them. *(Health and Safety Executive, Stress at Work (1995))*

This is the definition adopted in the rest of this book.

The fact remains, however, that there are grave difficulties in objectively assessing what stress is and, more particularly, how it affects different people. It is trite but true that what causes one person to experience stress to a level that leads to some form of a breakdown, whether physical or mental, may be viewed by another as a thrilling adrenalin rush. It is also true that attempts, most notably by the Health and Safety Executive, to develop standards for the management of workplace stress have met with difficulties because there is no universally applicable threshold at which stress becomes harmful to the health of all individuals: the propensity to suffer actual harm to health, in the form of physical or psychiatric illness, varies considerably from person to person, as does the level of stress necessary before this propensity becomes a reality.

This is one of the reasons why claims for compensation for workplace stress-related illnesses have been treated with such caution by courts and tribunals. The questions that have most troubled judges are that, if this is a question of highly individualised reactions to a range of workplace factors, then how can employers be expected to foresee which individuals may be at risk; what can employers reasonably do to eliminate or control that risk; and in what circumstances should they be held responsible for their failure to do so?

1.3 THE MOST COMMON SYMPTOMS OF STRESS

Stress can manifest itself in a range of different ways (physical, psychosocial and behavioural) and the symptoms will vary, depending on how long the individual continues to experience stress.

Short-term physical symptoms can include headaches, indigestion, high blood pressure, insomnia and frequent illness. Over the longer term, these symptoms can develop into conditions such as ulcers, asthma or heart disease. Everyone will react differently, but some research suggests that stress will have to continue for between five and 10 years before these serious conditions develop. (B.L. Anscheutz, 'The High Cost of Caring' November 1999.)

Psychosocial symptoms include, in the short term, anxiety, anger, apathy or irritability and can develop into full-blown depression and other psychiatric disorders.

Behavioural symptoms may include increased dependency on alcohol or other drugs, overeating or loss of appetite, poor job performance, neglect of responsibility and withdrawal or isolation from others.

1.4 THE SCOPE OF THE PROBLEM

The statistics suggest that the scope of the problem is potentially enormous. Estimates suggest that, in 2001, around 5 million employees believed that they were being exposed to workplace stress, with one in five describing their work as 'very' or 'extremely' stressful. Over half a million employees believed that they were experiencing workplace stress at levels that were making them ill. Of these, over 250,000 first became aware of stress-related symptoms in the preceding 12 months. It is not clear whether this is because levels of stress had in fact doubled over that period, or whether individuals have become more aware of stress as a workplace issue and therefore can identify and recognise the symptoms better.

The increase in the numbers of individuals complaining of workplace stress-related symptoms has been accompanied by an increase in the number of sick days. Self reported stress, depression or anxiety is estimated to have accounted for 13.5 million lost working days in 2001, with each affected individual taking, on average, 29 sick days. This can be compared with 6.5 million in the preceding 12 months. For every employee absent, however, it is safe to assume that there will be others who have not yet begun to take time off but who may be underperforming, or failing to discharge their duties because of stress-related symptoms.

1.5 THE MANAGEMENT IMPLICATIONS

As suggested at the outset, the management implications of high levels of workplace stress can cover operational, managerial and legal issues.

Operational

From an operational point of view problems could include:

- a large amount of absenteeism;
- poor performance by affected employees;
- increasing pressure on other employees;
- increased conflict between managers and other employees;
- fostering of climate ripe for bullying/harassment.

Managerial

Possible implications of workplace stress for management could include:

- handling increased complaints from employees about working conditions or other employees;
- handling resentment towards an affected employee, through perception that he is not pulling his weight;
- addressing resistance towards changes perceived to increase stress, e.g. moves towards greater profitability or productivity;
- tackling resistance from line managers who perceive their role as becoming increasingly difficult in the face of growing employee hostility;
- addressing an increase in unjustified absences, as employees perceive stress as an easy way to secure time off work without challenge.

Legal

The most likely legal implications are:

- potential for claims based in negligence for failing to prevent or reduce the risk of ill health due to workplace stress;
- employees suffering from stress-related illnesses (whether caused by workplace factors or not) may have a disability for the purposes of the Disability Discrimination Act 1995 and be entitled to reasonable adjustments to their working conditions;

- a climate of bullying and harassment can lead to legal claims based on stress or related illnesses;
- employers are under a duty to manage workplace stress in the same way as other workplace risks and a failure to do so could expose the employer to criminal prosecution as well as civil liability

1.6 CONCLUSION

There are, therefore, compelling commercial reasons why workplace stress should be viewed as a serious problem for both employees and employers alike. An understanding of the legal requirements and of the consequences of failing to tackle the problem can help an employer to develop strategies to address levels of stress which ultimately will benefit both employers and employees, as well as minimising the prospect of legal action.

For the legal adviser, it is imperative that the advice given to clients (whether employers or employees) is based on an under-standing of all the potentially relevant legal areas and what those mean in practice in terms of what each party can reasonably expect the other to do. In the chapters that follow, the various types of legal claim will be explored and the practical and management implications highlighted.

CHAPTER 2

The legal principles of negligence

2.1 INTRODUCTION

Since the decision of the High Court in *Walker* v. *Northumberland County Council* [1995] 1 All ER 737, it has been clear that, in certain circumstances, employers may be liable in negligence for stress-related illnesses suffered by employees as a result of conditions in the workplace. However, the question of precisely what those circumstances should be has remained fraught with controversy.

A review of the case law, both pre- and post-*Walker*, reveals inconsistencies in the approach adopted by the courts, leaving both employees and employers in some doubt as to the standards expected in the workplace. The Court of Appeal attempted to resolve these inconsistencies in *Hatton* v. *Sutherland* [2002] 2 All ER 1, with some, but by no means complete, success. In this chapter, the general legal principles relating to claims in negligence for stress-related illnesses will be examined and some of the problem areas analysed.

2.2 THE LEGAL ELEMENTS

It is accepted that the basic elements of a stress-related claim arising out of negligence are the same as in all claims in negligence:

1. There must be a duty to take care, i.e. the duty not to injure those that it might reasonably be foreseen will be harmed by negligent acts or omissions.
2. There must have been a failure to take such care as can reasonably be expected in the circumstances.
3. Damage must have been suffered as a result of that failure.

In the employment context, there is no doubt that an employer owes a duty of care to his employees. The scope of the duty is also clear:

it is to take reasonable care for the safety of employees and to take reasonable care to provide them with a safe system of work, a safe place of work and safe tools and equipment (see *Wilsons and Clyde Coal Co Limited* v. *English* [1938] AC 57).

It is important to remember that the duty is to take *reasonable* care. As was noted in *Walker*,

> the law does not impose upon [the employer] a duty of an insurer against all injury or damage caused by him however unlikely or unexpected and whatever the practical difficulties of guarding against it. It calls for no more than a reasonable response.

The point is an obvious one, but worth emphasising, as the demands of some employees complaining of stress-related symptoms and the reaction of some employers to such demands suggest that some may misunderstand the standards expected of employers in these circumstances.

As the Court of Appeal was quick to point out in *Hatton*, what is reasonable will depend on all the circumstances and the standards expected by the law should not be set too high. Instead, the standards should take into account commercial and economic considerations to avoid what the Court of Appeal described as 'an unfortunate and unwelcome effect on the employment market'.

2.3   APPLYING THE LEGAL ELEMENTS IN PRACTICE

Some problem areas

In claims arising out of workplace stress, the main difficulties arise in showing that the acts or omissions complained of were such that it was reasonably foreseeable that the employee might suffer harm.

The test is whether an employer can reasonably foresee that his conduct will expose the employee to the risk of personal injury. If it is reasonably foreseeable that an act or omission will expose an employee to the risk of physical harm (e.g. a failure to fit guards around dangerous parts of a machine), then, subject to causation and injury being established, an employer will be liable not just for the physical injury that follows, but also any attendant psychiatric harm (see *Page* v. *Smith* [1995] 2 All ER 736).

In stress-related claims, however, there are often no complaints that an employee was exposed to the risk of physical harm. Generally, the complaints relate to the nature or the extent of the workload, lack of management support or outright management hostility. In themselves, these are not factors that are likely to lead to direct physical harm. Whether or not it is reasonably foreseeable that they could lead to psychiatric harm is a question that the courts have approached with caution, for a number of reasons, including the following:

1. As has already been noted, the propensity to suffer psychiatric harm because of conditions in the workplace varies considerably from individual to individual. There is far less variation in the case of physical harm. An unguarded machine, for example, could be said to pose a similar risk to all, or at least most, individuals.

2. In deciding whether or not an individual is likely to suffer psychiatric harm, a number of questions arise, the answers to which may not be readily apparent to an employer. These are dealt with in the following three paragraphs.

Who knows what?

It goes without saying that an employer should know and understand the physical risks present in its undertaking. The same cannot be said of psychological risks. The employer will not necessarily know how an employee is going to react to, for example, pressures at work. The employer may also be unaware of events in the private life of the employee outside work, which may make that employee more susceptible to an adverse reaction to pressures within the workplace. These private pressures could include financial difficulties, marital breakdown, bereavement, or even alcohol and drug addiction. Without express notice of such issues, the employer will lack the information necessary to establish whether psychiatric harm is likely to be sustained.

What are the workplace factors that give rise to the risk of psychiatric harm and to what extent is the employer in control of them?

Again, an employer should be in control of the physical environment in its workplace. It may also be in control of some of the pressures that give rise to stress in the workplace, such as allocating workloads, or managing interpersonal conflict. However, it will not be in control of important contributory factors, such as how employees approach their work, how they prioritise tasks, what methods they use to manage their workloads and how good they are at managing their work/life balance.

Who is (or should be) responsible for keeping psychological risks in the workplace to a minimum?

The law has placed the responsibility for controlling and, if possible, eliminating workplace risks on the employer. However, the Courts have been quick to realise that psychological risks are different and should be treated differently. Psychological risks may be caused by many different factors and, on a practical level, the responsibility for doing something about them may be shared among many different categories of people – the employer, the employee, the employee's family, friends and other social contacts.

Causation

The second major problem area in stress-related claims is causation. Demonstrating that the damage suffered by the employee was as a result of the employer's negligent acts or omissions, rather than some extraneous factor in the employee's life, or some intrinsic susceptibility on the employee's part can prove to be an enormously contentious and difficult task.

A frequent complaint among employers is that many employees who complain of stress are undergoing some major upheaval in their private lives over which the employer has no control and for which the employer is understandably reluctant to accept responsibility. The courts have shown themselves to be sympathetic to the employer in such circumstances and have, in the past, accepted that the real cause of an employee's stress-related illness may be his own personality traits (see *Petch* v. *Customs and Excise Commissioners* [1993] ICR 789), events in the individual's personal life (see *Unwin* v. *West Sussex County Council* [2001] All ER(D) 180), a failure on the part of the employee to recognise that their health was suffering (see *Pratley* v. *Surrey County Council* [2002] EWHC 1608 (QB)), or an inability on the part of the employee to accept changing working practices. (see *Bishop* v. *Baker Refractories Limited* [2002] 2 All ER 1).

A final and important point (though not necessarily a problem area) that needs to be borne in mind throughout when dealing with stress-related claims in negligence is that the 'damage' complained of must be either a physical injury or illness (still comparatively rare in such claims) or a recognised psychiatric disorder. If the employee's symptoms fall short of a recognised disorder, then the employer will not be liable (see *Rorrison* v. *West Lothian College and Lothian*

Regional Council [2000] SCLR 245). General complaints of stress, anxiety, distress, sleeplessness and so on will not suffice, unless, together, they amount to some recognised disorder.

2.4 CONCLUSION

It is clear that applying the broad general tests for establishing liability in negligence to stress-related claims can give rise to many more questions than answers and it was against this background that the Court of Appeal gave its landmark decision in *Hatton*.

CHAPTER 3

Negligence in the wake of *Hatton* v. *Sutherland*

3.1 THE FACTS IN THE FOUR APPEALS

Before examining the Court of Appeal's decision, it is useful to consider the facts of the four appeals very briefly (*Hatton* v. *Sutherland, Barber* v. *Somerset Council, Jones* v. *Sandwell, Bishop* v. *Baker Refractories* [2002] 2 All ER 1). Some of the themes which emerge from these cases are good indicators of the kinds of workplace factors which may cause excessive levels of stress. In addition, claims based on work-related stress will often be highly fact sensitive, and it is useful to see what the Court of Appeal concluded to be the key factual elements necessary to substantiate a claim. The employees had been successful at first instance in all four cases: in all but one, the Court of Appeal overturned the first-instance decisions.

Hatton v. *Sutherland*

Penelope Hatton was employed as a modern languages teacher between 1980 and 1995. During that period, teaching and assessment methods changed dramatically, with a shift away from traditional exam-based assessment to a more modular system. Factors relevant to Mrs Hatton personally were that she was a single mother of two and that one of her children was suffering from an illness which required long-term hospitalisation.

In January 1994, around 18 months before she had a complete breakdown in her health, Mrs Hatton was attacked on the street. There was evidence that, towards the end of the period that she was employed at the school, she had many absences due to a number of different illnesses, some of which were stress-related.

Although Mrs Hatton sought to contend that her illness was caused by overwork, there was no evidence that she had complained to the school about the level of her workload at any time when she was employed by it. In fact, there was some evidence that, during the period immediately prior to her suffering her breakdown, her work-load had actually decreased. There was also some evidence that when she discussed her illnesses with her managers, she attributed her ill health to problems in her private life, rather than work. The Court of Appeal overturned the first-instance decision that the school should be liable for Mrs Hatton's illness.

Key issues for the Court of Appeal

- Mrs Hatton's pattern of absence and illness was on the face of it attributable to causes other than stress at work.
- There was no evidence of complaints about overwork.
- Although there had been changes in the way in which she was required to teach and/or assess over the period of her employment, most of these had been resolved by the time she suffered her final breakdown.
- Even if the breakdown had been foreseeable, there was no clear evidence as to the causes of the breakdown and what the school might have done to prevent it.

Barber v. *Somerset Council*

Alan Barber was an experienced maths teacher, who was appointed Head of Maths at his school in 1984 and remained at the school until November 1996, when he ceased work on medical grounds and he subsequently accepted early retirement in March 1997. The school in question was a comprehensive school in a deprived area and the number of pupils had halved between the mid-1980s and the mid-1990s. Resources had fallen accordingly and restructuring became essential. Mr Barber, in common with other heads of department, became an 'area of experience co-ordinator' in maths. He still had the same number of maths teachers, but the role of deputy heads of department, of which there had previously been two, was altered so that the individuals in those roles were given pastoral rather than management functions. To keep up his former salary level, Mr Barber took on additional responsibilities and there was unchallenged evidence that he was working long hours.

There was evidence that, generally, area of experience co-ordinators and the senior management team were having to work long hours at that time, particularly as the school was due for an

OFSTED inspection in 1996. The evidence did not indicate that Mr Barber was more overworked than any of his peers. There had been some complaints by Mr Barber about the level of his workload and the effects of the restructuring on his department in October 1995 and February 1996. In May 1996, he had three weeks off work with depression and gave evidence that he was surprised at this diagnosis, as he himself had not considered himself to be depressed.

On his return to work, he had meetings with his headmistress, whom the judge found was 'autocratic and bullying', but no significant changes to his working conditions were made. Mr Barber continued to suffer symptoms of stress over the summer holidays in 1996 and raised them with his doctor in October 1996. One of his managers had, by that stage, become somewhat concerned about Mr Barber and asked colleagues to keep an eye on him but, before anything more could be done, in November 1996, he lost control in the classroom and was advised to stop work immediately. The Court of Appeal overturned the first-instance finding that the school was liable for the psychiatric illness suffered by Mr Barber.

Key issues for the Court of Appeal

- Although there was some evidence that Mr Barber's illness was caused by stress at work, that did not necessarily mean that the school was in breach of duty or that its breach had caused the harm.
- It was clear that Mr Barber himself did not feel he was at risk of psychiatric illness before he was diagnosed with depression in May 1996.
- There was then a relatively short period whilst he was back at work before the summer holidays. Upon his return to work into the autumn term, there was then a very short period before he suffered a second breakdown.
- It was, therefore, difficult to identify a point at which the school had a duty to take steps to help Mr Barber. In addition, given the speed at which the final breakdown occurred, it was difficult to see what positive steps the school could have taken to help Mr Barber.

Jones v. *Sandwell*

Olwen Jones was employed as an administrative assistant at a local authority training centre between August 1992 and January 1995, when she went off sick with anxiety and depression. There was evidence that her position was a new post and that she was having to work grossly excessive hours, over the 37 per week required by her contract of employment. She complained of overwork to her immediate managers from an early stage and also complained to more senior management of bullying by her immediate managers. There were promises that additional resources would be provided to Mrs Jones, but none of these were forthcoming. There was also evidence that a complaint made by Mrs Jones, of discrimination and harassment by her immediate managers, which had affected her health, was not properly addressed.

Mrs Jones did not take any time off work sick during any of the time she was employed and there was no specific medical event which might have alerted her employers to the risk of the breakdown, which occurred in January 1995. The Court of Appeal upheld with 'some hesitation' the original finding that the council was liable for the breakdown which Mrs Jones subsequently suffered.

Key issues for the Court of Appeal

- The job that Mrs Jones was asked to do was one which made unreasonable demands upon an employee in a comparatively junior grade.
- The management response to her complaints was itself unreasonable.
- There were complaints about her workload which were taken sufficiently seriously for extra help to be promised twice, but no help was in fact provided.
- It was not difficult to identify what steps the council could have taken to prevent the injury which in fact occurred: the promised help which never materialised was a relevant factor.

Bishop v. Baker Refractories Limited

Melvyn Bishop was employed by Baker Refractories Limited between 1979 and February 1997, when he had a nervous breakdown and attempted suicide. In 1992, the company was taken over by an American company and reorganisation began. New shift patterns were introduced in 1994 and work was reorganised so that employees were required to do a greater variety of tasks. In general, the new shifts and changes in working patterns were welcomed by the employees, but not by Mr Bishop. He complained about the changes to his manager, and another employee separately expressed his concerns that Mr Bishop was not coping. Unfortunately, Mr Bishop's old job was no longer available and there was, therefore, little that could be done to accommodate the changes that Mr Bishop wanted.

In terms of Mr Bishop's health, he was told by his GP to change his job in November 1996, but he did not discuss this with his employers. Immediately prior to his nervous breakdown, he had some three weeks away from work, some of which was time when he would have been off shift in any event and other times when he was ill. His breakdown occurred on 25 February 2003. The Court of Appeal overturned the first-instance finding that the employer was liable for the illness suffered by Mr Bishop.

Key issues for the Court of Appeal

- There was nothing unusual, excessive or unreasonable about the demands which had been placed upon Mr Bishop by his work.
- The real cause of Mr Bishop's problem was his inability to cope with change.
- Mr Bishop had failed to act on the advice of his own doctor.
- The employer was not told of the advice given to him by his doctor in November 1996.
- The short period of absence and the sickness notes which supported it in 1997 were not sufficient to alert the employer to the fact that something needed to be done.
- There was, in any event, nothing that the employer could reasonably do: the job that Mr Bishop wanted was no longer available.

3.2 *HATTON* v. *SUTHERLAND*: THE COURT OF APPEAL'S DECISION

In allowing all but one of the appeals, the Court of Appeal took the approach of adopting what it described as 16 practical propositions and then applying these to the facts summarised above. The propositions are a useful checklist for both employers and employees to assess the strengths and weaknesses of any putative claim. They also offer useful proactive guidance for employers and employees alike as to how attempts to manage stress-related problems in the workplace are likely to be interpreted in any subsequent negligence action. However, as will be seen, despite the Court of Appeal's efforts, several problem areas remain.

3.3 THE COURT OF APPEAL'S PRACTICAL PROPOSITIONS

1. *The ordinary principles of employers' liability apply to claims for psychiatric (or physical) illness or injury caused by work-related stress.*

2. *The threshold question is: was this kind of harm reasonably foreseeable to the employee?*

   Two points are of particular note here. First, the Court of Appeal expressly rejected the argument that employers were under any general duty to their employees as a group to prevent psychiatric illness caused by work-related stress. Rather, the duty extended only to individual employees who were at risk. There was, therefore, no question of it being reasonably foreseeable that all employees might suffer psychiatric harm because, for example, of the way that the employer conducted its undertaking, but only of it being reasonably foreseeable that a particular individual might suffer harm because of facts peculiar to him.

   This will no doubt come as something of a blow to those who have tried to argue that a general failure to take steps to control or eliminate workplace stress should be sufficient evidence of negligence to render an employer liable to any individual who has suffered illness as a result. The Court of Appeal's approach also does not sit well with the approach that employers are expected to adopt by the Health and Safety Executive (HSE), considered in more detail in **Chapter 5**. For present purposes, it is sufficient to note that the HSE takes the view that the potential risks to the health of all employees from workplace stress should be assessed and controlled in broadly the same way as any other risks. Employers who follow the HSE's advice and carry out proactive risk assessments will have worked on the assumption that there are factors in the workplace that could adversely affect the mental health of all their employees. It may, therefore, be harder for these employers to argue subsequently that they did not foresee the risk of harm to any particular individual.

   Secondly, the kind of harm that the Court of Appeal felt had to be reasonably foreseeable was an injury to health attributable to stress at work. It is not enough that it is reasonably foreseeable to an employer that an employee is being exposed to occupational stress. It must be reasonably foreseeable that an employee is being exposed to the risk of harm to his health because of occupational stress.

3. *Foreseeability depends on what the employer actually knows or ought to know.*

   The Court of Appeal focused on what the employer knew or ought to have known about two things: first, the particular characteristics of the employee; and second, the nature of the work carried out by the employee, including any demands placed on him by the employer.

   Relevant characteristics of the employee include:

   - any known pre-existing problems;
   - any sudden and unexplained absences; or
   - any uncharacteristic decline in performance;

   provided that these are or may be attributable to work-related stress, rather than any other cause.

   The presence of these characteristics may be sufficient to put the employer on notice that an employee's health is at risk.

   The nature of the work carried out by the employee may also be relevant, though not necessarily decisive. It may be more foreseeable that an overworked employee in an intellectually or emotionally demanding job is at risk of injury to his health, than somebody who is doing a job that is well within their capabilities. However, in the absence of any other signs, it appears to be inconsistent with the Court of Appeal's overall approach for the nature of the work alone to be a sufficient basis for liability.

4. *The test is the same, irrespective of the kind of employment.*

   In formulating this proposition, the Court of Appeal expressly rejected the argument that some professions were intrinsically more dangerous to mental health than others, although the type of work could be a relevant factor in deciding whether it was reasonably foreseeable that a particular individual was at risk of injury to health. Two of the cases before the court involved teachers and it had been submitted that the defendants in those cases ought to have known that teachers generally were at risk of developing psychiatric illnesses due to work-related stress, because of the prevalence of complaints and claims in the sector. The court disagreed. It had, as previously stated, rejected the idea that there was any duty to prevent psychiatric harm to employees as a class, but rather only to particular employees, who, for whatever reason, were known or suspected to be at risk. It was not the job, the court concluded, but rather the interaction between the individual and the job which causes the harm.

5. *Relevant factors in deciding whether harm to health was reasonably foreseeable include the nature and extent of work, signs from other employees and signs from the employee in question.*

When looking at the nature and/or extent of work, pertinent questions include:

- whether the job is intellectually or emotionally demanding;
- whether it routinely calls for excessive hours; or
- whether other excessive demands are placed on the employee by the employer.

Placing unreasonable demands on an employee and then responding unreasonably to complaints about those demands might be sufficient to put the employer on notice that there was a risk of injury to health.

Relevant signs from other employees could include:

- a history of stress-related ill health in the same department;
- absenteeism where there is reason to believe that it is linked to work-related stress; or
- complaints from other members of the same team or department.

However, in view of the Court of Appeal's overall reluctance to accept that any job poses an equal risk of psychological injury to all employees, it is likely that the third factor – signs from the employee himself – will be most decisive in determining liability. In the absence of any such evidence, it is likely that the evidence relating to the factors set out above will have to be overwhelming before an employer is held to be liable.

What signs from an employee should employers be wary of? The main warning sign ought to be any express warnings about harm to psychological health because of stress in the workplace, whether those emanate from the employee himself or from the employee's medical advisers. This does raise an interesting question about the weight that employers should attach to general practitioners' certificates and/or notes. A frequent complaint from employers is about the sheer volume of such notes that they receive. Many will simply state that the employee is 'stressed', or even 'too tired for work'. In themselves these cannot be said to be diagnoses of any medical condition, but will they be sufficient to satisfy the Court of Appeal's requirement of a warning about harm to health? A suggested solution to the problem can be found in **Chapter 10**.

It is important to remember that general complaints from the employee about working conditions, or that the work is too difficult or demanding, are unlikely to be deemed sufficient to render it reasonably foreseeable that an employee's health will suffer, unless, presumably, there is overwhelming evidence of this from some other source. One such source might be empirical evidence that an employee's health is being adversely affected: sudden or unexplained absences from work, for example, but only if there is reason to believe that such absences are linked to workplace stress rather than any other cause.

6. *An employer is generally entitled to take what an employee says at face value, unless there is good reason to the contrary.*

This particular proposition was broken down by the Court of Appeal into two parts. First, unless an employer knows of some particular problem or vulnerability, then it is entitled to assume that an employee is up to the normal pressures of the job. Secondly, an employer is under no duty to make searching enquiries of its employees, but can, as the proposition says, take what it is told at face value.

An employer may, of course, know of an employee's particular vulnerability through having seen medical records, having carried out health surveillance, or having made other enquiries. In light of the Court of Appeal's decision, the temptation may, in future, be to make fewer enquiries, or to take fewer steps to establish the state of an employee's mental health. However, there is a need for caution on the part of employers. As set out under 5. above, there may be circumstances in which an employer is expected to infer that what it has been told is not the full story or the true story. In addition, other legal requirements may preclude this kind of wholly reactive and passive approach – see for example the requirements of the Disability Discrimination Act 1995 in **Chapter 6**.

It may seem to many that, in putting the burden so firmly on employees to notify the employer that they are experiencing problems with work-related stress, the Court of Appeal was to an extent blinding itself to the realities of the situation. The commercial reality of the situation is that many employees may be afraid to speak out because they fear losing their jobs or missing out on promotion prospects. The medical reality in some cases is that the last person to know that there is a problem is the employee concerned.

It may be because of a desire to mitigate this potentially harsh result that the way that the Court of Appeal dealt overall with foreseeability in stress-related claims betrays a certain hesitancy. On the one hand, it is clear that the court was sympathetic to employers and keen to close what might otherwise have been a floodgate of such claims. On the other, the Court of Appeal has left sufficient ambiguities to leave employers who fail to spot what, with hindsight, may appear to be obvious signs at some risk.

7. *To trigger a duty to take steps, the signs of impending harm to health must be plain enough for a reasonable employer to do something about it.*

    It is likely that many disputes in the future will focus on whether or not the signs of harm to health were sufficiently plain to trigger a duty on the part of the employer to take some action. The Court of Appeal declined to limit the test to 'clear and unequivocal signs of an impending breakdown'. Again, presumably, the Court of Appeal felt that the question could be answered by considering the cogency of the evidence in the three areas referred to in 5. above: the nature and extent of work, any signs from other employees and any signs from the employee himself.

8. *An employer will only be in breach of duty if he fails to take steps which are reasonable in the circumstances.*

    As is clear from 1.–7. above, in future, employees may struggle to overcome the various hurdles in showing that it was or ought to have been reasonably foreseeable that they were at risk of harm to health because of exposure to workplace stress. Even those who can demonstrate this will not necessarily be successful in a claim of negligence. A claim will only succeed if the employee can identify steps that it would have been reasonable for the employer to take which the employer failed to take. In any claim, the onus will be on the employee to identify what steps he feels could or should have been taken and for the employer to raise arguments as to why those steps were not reasonable in all the circumstances.

    The next four propositions set out the approach that courts should follow in deciding whether or not there were steps that the employer could reasonably have taken once it became aware of the risk of harm to the employee's health.

9. *The particular characteristics of the employer's operation are relevant in deciding what steps were or would have been reasonable.*

The Court of Appeal made it clear that the question of reasonableness in this context could not be decided without reference to the particular undertaking in question. Relevant issues include the size of the organisation and its resources and whether it is a public sector or a private sector undertaking. There appeared to be an implicit acknowledgement by the Court of Appeal that it might be reasonable for a public sector employer to take more action to help employees that it had identified as being at risk of harm to help, than a small, private sector undertaking.

Other relevant issues include the demands that the undertaking faces, such as the needs of other employees. This 'catch all' category could prove a fruitful area for employers in the future. Why limit matters to the demands and needs of other employees? Will commercial needs and demands not be equally relevant? It is arguable that the process of change in the workplace (restructuring, downsizing and repositioning in the market place, for example) is one of the major causes of workplace stress. The associated changes in working patterns, such as job redefinition, can lead to overwork or interpersonal conflict, which are frequently cited as the causes of illness. Yet, the Court of Appeal was alive to the fact that the commercial reality is that such changes are necessary in order for businesses to survive and for the economy to thrive. Will employers be able to rely on these commercial factors in the future?

Another area that employers may find useful to exploit is the requirements of any statutory or regulatory framework within which they operate. In the *Barber* case, one of the factors that added significantly to the stress to which Mr Barber was exposed was an OFSTED inspection. It is difficult to see what the school in that case could have done to minimise this stress, which was caused by a mandatory and externally imposed requirement. The weight of 'red tape' that is the subject of many complaints from businesses will, in reality, fall on the shoulders of individual employees. It may in fact be the case that, because the requirement is imposed by Government, the courts have no choice but to accept that businesses must comply with it, however stressful it may prove to be for employees.

10. *Not only must the employee show that the employer failed to take steps it could reasonably be expected to take, the employee must also show that those steps would have done the employee some good.*

This is a significant point. The Court of Appeal identified the need for employees in future claims to adduce expert evidence to show that the steps that the employee wanted to see taken would in fact have done some good. The court accepted that it can often be difficult to know what would have done enough good to make a real difference to the eventual outcome as far as the employee was concerned and so this could be a real problem area for employees in future claims.

There may be some cases where it will be relatively straightforward to identify what steps would have assisted the claimant employee. In *Lancaster* v. *Birmingham City Council* [1999] 6 QR 4, for example, the claimant was able to show that she had been moved from a position that she had held for many years to a new and very different one without any additional training or support.

In other cases, claimant employees have been able to point to unresolved complaints or grievances as key opportunities missed by the employer to arrest the employee's decline into psychiatric illness. It is likely to be easier for an employee whose claim is based on allegations of bullying by management to point to steps that might have helped him than for one whose principal complaint is overwork. The former can suggest practical solutions, such as redeployment or a change in immediate line management, whilst the latter is left with more abstract suggestions, such as a reduction in workload (when should it have happened and how big a reduction would have helped?) or a sabbatical.

11. *An employer who offers a confidential advice service and referral to appropriate counselling is unlikely to be in breach of the duty to take steps.*

This is arguably one of the most controversial of the Court of Appeal's propositions. It has, unsurprisingly perhaps, been seized on by some employers as their insurance policy against future claims. On the face of it, it does appear to offer a straightforward solution to the problem of ill health caused by workplace stress. In reality, however, it is difficult to see how counselling alone, without any attempt to resolve the root causes of the problem, will prevent or minimise the risk of illness. For example, an employee who is suffering an adverse reaction to excessive demands from an unsympathetic, perhaps even bullying, manager is unlikely to derive much benefit from an hour's counselling a week if he is then required to return to precisely those same conditions.

Employers who rely too heavily on this particular proposition may, in any event, find themselves falling foul of other legal requirements, for example under the health and safety legislation (see **Chapter 5**).

12. *If the only effective step would be to dismiss or demote, an employer will not be in breach of duty for allowing a willing employee to continue with the job.*

The Court of Appeal accepted that, taken to its logical conclusion, this proposition could be taken to justify the most unsafe working practices. However, it appears to be a natural consequence of the court's earlier finding that, as far as psychological risks were concerned, there was no such thing as an inherently unsafe job, or inherently unsafe working practice. It was, therefore, prepared to leave the onus on the employee to decide whether he could carry on with the job, or whether he should leave.

It appears that, in arriving at this decision, the Court of Appeal was influenced by the similar approach taken to physical risks in the case of *Withers* v. *Perry Chain Co Limited* [1961] 1 WLR 1314, where the court had concluded that it could not 'believe that the common law requires employers to refuse to employ a person who is willing to work for them simply because they think that it is not in the person's best interests to do the work'.

The decision in *Withers* was recently considered in *Coxall* v. *Goodyear Great Britain Limited* [2002] IRLR 742, CA, which involved a claimant with occupational asthma who argued that he should have been moved to other employment or, as a last resort, dismissed, rather than being allowed to continue with work that exacerbated his condition. The Court of Appeal concluded that there was clear and compelling medical evidence that the employee should not be allowed to continue working and that the employer's failure to follow the medical advice was negligent, notwithstanding the employee's willingness to continue and the *Withers* principle. The Court of Appeal also concluded that the employee's own willingness to continue in these circumstances might amount to contributory negligence, warranting a reduction in damages. Nevertheless, it may be that if there is compelling medical evidence that an employee is at risk of exacerbating a psychiatric condition by continuing in his current employment, the employer ought to consider dismissal, subject of course to issues of breach of contract and unfair dismissal (see **Chapter 8**).

13. *In all cases, there is a need to identify with precision the steps that the employer could or should have taken.*

    As stated at 8. above, in a claim in negligence, the onus is on the employee as the claimant to identify what steps the employer should have taken, when those steps should have been taken and to show that they would have done the employee some good. The Court of Appeal betrayed some frustration at some of the first instance decisions in this regard, where the employer had been found liable on the basis that the risk of harm to the health of the claimant employee had been reasonably foreseeable, and the employee had sustained some form of psychiatric illness, without directing their minds to the question of what the employer could reasonably have done to prevent the illness.

14. *The employee must show that the employer's breach of the duty to take steps caused the harm, not just that the harm was caused by workplace stress.*

    It is important to remember that, in the context of negligence, the employer's duty is *not* to take steps to prevent stress in the workplace (which can be contrasted with the duty under health and safety legislation in **Chapter 5**), but rather, where it can reasonably be foreseen that an employee's health is at risk because of workplace stress, to take reasonable steps to prevent or minimise that injury to health.

15. *Where the harm has more than one cause, the employer will only be liable for that proportion which is attributable to its wrongdoing.*

    Although on the face of it, this is a self-evident proposition, in practice it could be very hard to apportion liability in this way. Stress-related illnesses can be complex in terms of causation, as they may depend on an individual's reaction to many factors. The Court of Appeal accepted that this meant that apportionment was likely to have to be a fairly 'broad brush' exercise.

16. *Damages will take into account any pre-existing disorder and the chance that the employee may have succumbed to the illness in any event.*

    The question of pre-existing conditions is one which comes up again and again. Many employers feel that they should not be held liable where the cause of an employee's condition pre-dates the employment or is not employment related. To a large extent, that is correct. However, a pre-existing condition or history of psychiatric illness should not be ignored, for two reasons. First, they are key issues in determining the likelihood that someone's health may suffer if they are exposed to excessive pressures in the workplace, irrespective of the cause of that earlier or pre-existing condition. Secondly, once an employer is aware of the condition, then, whatever its cause, the employer comes under a duty not to exacerbate or aggravate it (see *Unwin* v. *West Sussex County Council* [2001] All ER(D) 180).

If, however, an employer's real 'sin' is to have exacerbated or aggravated a pre-existing condition, then the employer will only be held liable for the effect of that exacerbation, not of the underlying condition itself. In *Unwin*, for example, it was held that the claimant's underlying condition meant that she would have been unfit to continue in her current employment at some stage in the near future, even without her employer's negligence. The employer's negligence had only speeded up her retirement due to ill health and the claimant was only entitled to modest damages for that.

3.4 CONCLUSION

As can be seen from the above, significant problem areas remain for both employees and employers when dealing with claims in negligence arising out of work-related ill health, despite the Court of Appeal's attempts to clarify matters. In **Chapter 4**, the practical implications of the Court of Appeal's guidelines will be examined.

CHAPTER 4

Claims in negligence

4.1 APPLYING THE LAW IN PRACTICE

The law as outlined in **Chapters 2** and **3** can be of practical use to both employers and employees who are experiencing difficulties with stress in the workplace. Not only can it be used to assess the strengths and weaknesses of any threatened claim, thus enabling the parties to conduct any settlement negotiations in a proper context, but it can also be used at an earlier stage to decide whether working conditions need to be adjusted to minimise the risk of a successful claim.

Examples of the practical assistance that the law can give include, from the employer's perspective, the ability to distinguish genuine from non-genuine cases. For an employee who has made repeated requests for specific assistance against the backdrop of letters from medical advisers warning of increasing health problems, reasonable changes to working patterns or other suitable steps should, applying the Court of Appeal's guidelines, be considered, whilst a more robust approach can perhaps be taken with employees whose complaints lack the cogency and the detail deemed to be necessary to lead to a successful claim. By the same token, employees who are dissatisfied with their employer's handling of their complaints about workplace stress may want to consider what further they can do in accordance with the guidelines to draw their plight to their employer's attention.

4.2 APPLYING THE PRACTICAL PROPOSITIONS

In the first part of this chapter, the use of the guidelines as a management tool is explored whilst, in the second, applying the law to decide how to trade putative claims is considered.

Whilst the guidelines can no doubt be of practical assistance to both employers and employees, there is a need to sound a note of caution. As has been made clear in **Chapter 3**, the approach recommended by the Court of Appeal does not necessarily sit well with other legal requirements. There is a need to consider all the areas identified in this book before deciding how to act. Provided that this caveat is borne in mind, applying the principles and guidance relevant to the law in negligence can assist as outlined below.

4.3 CHECKLISTS TO AID MANAGEMENT IN COMPLAINTS OF WORKPLACE STRESS

The Court of Appeal's practical propositions can be used as a checklist to establish whether action to assist any particular employee complaining of stress should be taken.

Is the risk of psychiatric harm to the employee foreseeable?

Question	Yes	No
1. Has the employee complained about work-related stress?		
2. Is this the first complaint?		
3. Is there any express warning that the employee's health is suffering?		
4. Is there any other reason to suspect health problems due to workplace stress, e.g. unexplained and unusual absences?		
5. Does the employee have any history of psychiatric problems?		
6. Is the employee suffering from any known pre-existing condition?		
7. Are there known incidents of ill health due to workplace stress amongst the other employees in the same team or department?		
8. Have there been other complaints about workplace stress from the team or department?		
9. What kind of work is the employee doing?		

	Yes	No
10. Have there been any recent changes, such as increased demands in terms of workload or responsibilities?		
11. Is there evidence that the employee is working significantly harder or longer or is facing significantly more demanding targets than his colleagues?		

Remember that the Court of Appeal was keen to put a good deal of responsibility on the employee to draw any problems he is experiencing to the employer's attention, so the starting point will usually be a complaint (either informal or formal) from the employee himself. However, the Court of Appeal also recognised that there may be circumstances where it should have been obvious to the employer that there were problems, even without any express complaints. It may, therefore, be that the starting point will be question 4 in the table above.

Positive answers to the majority of the questions above should be taken as indicators that the risk of harm to health may be foreseeable, although, clearly, further investigations will be needed before foreseeability can be decisively established.

What steps can the employer reasonably take to help the employee?

Once the risk of harm is deemed to be foreseeable, consideration should be given to establishing what steps the employer can take to avoid or minimise the harm suffered. The steps need to be reasonable, having regard to the particular characteristics of the employer, and there needs to be a reasonable prospect of the steps doing the employee some good. The following checklist may assist:

Question	Yes	No
1. Are there any steps that the employee is requesting should be taken to avoid harm to health, or improve or prevent a deterioration of his condition?		
2. Is there reason to think that these steps will in fact assist the employee: is there medical evidence, or credible evidence from the employee to this effect?		

31

Question	Yes	No
3. Can these steps be accommodated by the employer: consider, for example, the cost, disruption to other employees, needs of customers/regulators?		
4. Is there anything else the employer could reasonably offer to do, again considering factors such as cost, disruption to other employees and so on?		
5. Is it likely that expert medical/occupational health assistance will help to decide what steps might assist the employee?		
6. What arrangements are to be made to ensure that any agreed steps are being followed by (a) the employee, (b) other employees in the team/department, and (c) the employee's supervisors and/or line managers.		

The first step ought to be to speak to the employee: he may have a good idea as to what adaptations to working conditions are necessary. It is sometimes the case that employers are reluctant to discuss such matters with employees, often through a fear that they will then be forced to act on anything that the employee tells them or any requests that are made. Anecdotal evidence suggests that some employees may have unrealistic expectations of what an employer is obliged to do to prevent harm to their mental health or to accommodate their condition: some requests amount to a demand for continued payment/employment without any real duties at all. It should be remembered that the employer needs only to take reasonable action and is not obliged to agree to unduly onerous or disproportionately expensive demands. Merely asking an employee for suggestions does not commit the employer to agreeing to unreasonable requests. On the contrary, showing an open attitude and a willingness to assist, if possible, is likely to stand the employer in good stead in any future claim by the employee.

There may be cases where the employee is unable to suggest action that might assist and expert advice is needed, either from the employer's occupational health team, or from the employee's medical adviser. In some cases, it may be necessary to consult an adviser who is independent of both parties.

It is important to establish that the suggested steps will go some way towards resolving the reported problems. To use an obvious example, a re-allocation of workloads (if practicable) may assist an employee who reports sleeplessness, anxiety or depression because of overwork. However, the same action is unlikely to assist an employee who is complaining about bullying or harassment in the workplace. Similarly, workplace adjustments may not assist an employee where the real cause of the stress is not work-related.

If steps are agreed, then arrangements should also be made to ensure that those steps are implemented and that their continued efficacy is regularly monitored. Care should be taken to ensure that the employee's line managers and/or supervisors comply with any action that they are required to take and that other employees do not prevent or adversely affect the implementation of the agreed measures. If, for example, the employer has accepted the view of the employee's medical adviser that the employee is fit to return to or to continue to work provided that he takes certain medication and undertakes lighter duties for a period, then the relevant line manager needs to ensure that the employee is not given additional duties or prevented from taking the medication. Other employees may feel aggrieved or resentful at what they perceive to be favourable treatment towards the employee in question: their reaction can add pressure and become a new source of stress for the employee. These are difficult issues, but issues which need to be managed. Suggestions as to how to manage these problems can be found in **Chapter 10**.

Particular care should be taken with employees who are known to be suffering from a pre-existing psychiatric condition, whether that be work related or not. In particular, if arrangements are made to allow the employee to continue to work, or to return to work, then not only must care be taken to ensure that those arrangements are in fact put into place, but care must also be taken to monitor the effectiveness of those arrangements in preventing any return or exacerbation of the employee's condition.

In *Young* v. *The Post Office* [2002] IRLR 660, the employer agreed a return to work on flexible terms and there was no evidence that any pressure was put on the employee in breach of those agreed terms. The employee failed to avail himself of the flexibility offered and the employer was still held liable for a recurrence of the employee's condition when the employee suffered a relapse. The Court of Appeal refused to overturn the first-instance finding that, on the employee's return to work, the employer was under a duty to monitor the employee's workload more proactively and so was liable for the relapse when it could not show that it had taken steps to monitor what the employee did on his return. Merely relying on the employee to raise concerns was not sufficient. The decision is all the more notable for the fact that the relapse occurred a matter of weeks after the employee returned to work.

4.4 CHECKLIST TO PREPARE A POTENTIAL CLAIM IN NEGLIGENCE BY AN EMPLOYEE

The practical propositions identified by the Court of Appeal can assist in assessing the merits of any potential claim in negligence by an employee and can also assist in deciding what evidence is needed to support the claim.

The starting point will be to establish that the employee has suffered a recognised psychiatric illness. For further guidance on what constitutes a recognised disorder in the context of mental health, see **Chapter 6**.

Good, but objective, medical evidence is necessary and a general practitioner's note is unlikely to be sufficient. Further, in a number of the reported cases, criticism has been made over reliance by the employee's expert on, for example, the employee's own version of events. In the current climate, with the withdrawal of legal aid for such cases, the need to get expert medical evidence early to assess whether or not there is any claim to be brought can result in fairly high costs being incurred at the outset, without any guarantee of success. Further, expert evidence may be needed before the employee can be advised that he has a claim: a single, joint expert may not therefore be a viable option.

The next step is to consider what evidence is available to show that the risk of illness was reasonably foreseeable to the employer. This will involve gathering evidence on the nature and extent of the job, including any evidence of excessive working hours, emotionally demanding work, demanding deadlines or targets, or a particularly challenging management style. Useful evidence may also be gleaned by considering the culture of the organisation: how are complaints handled and how do people interrelate with one another? The aim for the employee's legal advisers should be to build up a picture of an 'unhealthy' working environment.

Supporting evidence may be found through interviewing others in the same or similar jobs, particularly others who have suffered ill health in the same team or department. There may be evidence that other employees have complained, or have raised concerns about the demands of the job in exit interviews, disciplinary or grievance procedures.

Finally, there is a need to focus on the evidence of the employee himself. The employee's legal advisers should be looking for documented complaints about working conditions and the risk of harm to health. If these are not present, then this could significantly adversely affect the chances of a successful claim.

There was suggestion by the Court of Appeal that expert evidence might assist in deciding whether all the evidence suggested above taken together would make it reasonably foreseeable to an employer that the individual in question was likely to suffer harm to health. Ultimately, as this will be a question of fact in every case, it is difficult to see how expert evidence could assist.

If there is evidence that it was or should have been foreseeable to the employer that the employee was at risk of illness, the employee's legal advisers should identify what steps it would have been reasonable for the employer to take. Evidence on this point could be gathered from a number of sources, including the following.

Question	Yes	No
1. Were any complaints or grievances by the individual wrongly dismissed, or not followed through? (It may be that if a complaint or grievance had been handled properly and appropriate action taken at that stage, then some of the employee's later problems could have been avoided.)		
2. Has the employee been treated differently from any others in the undertaking?		
3. Is there any industry guidance setting out the types of steps that employers in that sector could take? The Engineering Employers' Federation and the Association of Colleges, to name but two, have issued standard guidance on the management of stress in the workplace for businesses in their sectors.		
4. Has the employer failed to take any steps recommended by the Health and Safety Executive?		
5. Does the size and/or the resources of the undertaking suggest that more could have been done than was in fact done to assist the employee?		

A final, but important, piece of evidence that the employee must put forward is that those steps would have helped to prevent or mitigate the harm which was ultimately suffered. This may be difficult to do and will undoubtedly require the assistance of an appropriate expert.

4.5 CHECKLIST IN SUPPORT OF A DEFENCE TO A CLAIM BY AN EMPLOYEE

Those advising employers can also use the practical propositions to identify the vulnerable elements of any claim put forward by an employee. The following points may be relevant.

Question	Yes	No
1. What is the ill treatment complained of by the employee?		
2. Is it particularly lengthy, perhaps extended over a long period of time or stale? (If so, there may be an argument that the employee should have acted before he did.)		
3. Has the employee given any previous warnings or complaints about the level of work and the risk to health?		
4. Is there any corroborating evidence for the claim from colleagues or others?		
5. Were there any observable warning signs such as absenteeism or a drop in performance?		
6. Were there any changes in terms of the employee's working conditions which can be linked to the onset of the symptoms complained of?		
7. Is there a grievance procedure which the employee could have made use of? Is there evidence that the grievance procedure has been used and operated satisfactorily in other similar cases?		
8. Does the employer have an open-door policy to occupational health and human resources, of which the employee has failed to avail himself?		
9. Is there a past history of any psychiatric illness or depression? If so, can it be argued this should lead to a reduction in damages, as the employee may well have suffered a recurrence of the condition in any event?		
10. Is anything known about the employee's private life which may have caused or contributed to the illness complained of?		

4.6   CONCLUSION

Although there are still a number of grey areas in terms of claims for workplace stress, the Court of Appeal's checklist should go some way towards making it easier to identify those cases which are likely to succeed and enable an early assessment of the merits to take place before significant costs have been incurred.

CHAPTER 5

Health and safety

5.1 INTRODUCTION

At one time, the application of the statutory framework governing health and safety at work to issues surrounding workplace stress might have been viewed as contentious. For the most part, since the introduction of the current regime in 1974, the focus had (in the opinion of many, rightly) been focused on eliminating and/or minimising risks to the physical safety of employees. However, since the early 1990s, the Health and Safety Executive (HSE) has increasingly expounded the view that the duties imposed under the health and safety regime include a duty in respect of an employee's psychological health and welfare as much as a duty in respect of his physical safety and welfare.

The HSE has offered much guidance and advice over the last decade or so as to how workplace stress should be managed to discharge an employer's duties in this regard. It is clear, however, that even the HSE recognises that there are problems in applying the traditional health and safety approach. The guidance has fallen short of mandatory requirements, such as an Approved Code of Practice or specific legislation governing the subject, and this may well be a reflection of the practical difficulties in applying the same degree of certainty to measures designed to eliminate or control workplace stress as to those designed to eliminate or control physical risks present in the workplace.

Similarly, the HSE has not, to date, authorised or sanctioned the use of any of the many enforcement measures available to it against employers who have failed to take steps to manage workplace stress. This may change in the future, particularly if the HSE succeeds in its aim of developing a series of accepted management standards in relation to workplace stress. Once these are in place, failure by an employer to achieve the necessary standards or put in place the recommended measures will make it easier to identify a relevant failure, which should lead to prosecution and/or other enforcement activity.

Finally, in terms of civil liability, the relevance of measures to eliminate or control workplace stress may increase with the proposed change to the Management of Health and Safety at Work Regulations, to remove the current civil liability exclusion.

This chapter explores the issues in greater detail, considers the impact they have on an employer's legal obligations in relation to employees who develop stress-related illnesses and also considers the extent to which the regime offers practical guidance which can be applied to manage workplace stress on a day-to-day basis.

5.2   THE BASIC DUTIES

A number of pieces of health and safety legislation are relevant to the issue of workplace stress, as follows:

- Health and Safety at Work etc. Act 1974;
- Management of Health and Safety at Work Regulations 1999, SI 1999/3242;
- Working Time Regulations 1998, SI 1998/1833.

Issues arising out of the Working Time Regulations are dealt with in **Chapter 9.**

Health and Safety at Work etc. Act 1974

Under s.2(1) of the Health and Safety at Work etc. Act 1974, employers are under a duty to ensure, so far as is reasonably practicable, the health, safety and welfare of employees at work. As indicated above, historically this provision was interpreted narrowly so as to relate principally to physical workplace risks. However, the HSE now takes the view that the provision is equally applicable to psychological risks and requires the implementation of measures to prevent stress-related illnesses as a result of a variety of factors connected with the workplace or the type of work.

Management of Health and Safety at Work Regulations 1999

Regulation 3 of the Management of Health and Safety at Work Regulations requires every employer to make a 'suitable and sufficient assessment' of the risks to the health and safety of its employees to which they are exposed whilst at work. In this context, workplace stress may be relevant in one of two ways. First, it can be considered to pose a workplace risk which requires assessment in its own right and, secondly, it can be a workplace factor which increases or alters the risks posed to employees by other workplace conditions, because employees who are experiencing stress may react differently to those workplace conditions.

The remainder of this chapter will explore the implications of these duties in greater detail. It is useful to bear in mind that the HSE's practical interpretation of these duties is that an employer must make sure that its employees are not made ill by their work. This is a broad approach to the question of workplace stress and related illnesses, particularly when compared with the very narrow approach taken by the Court of Appeal in *Hatton* v. *Sutherland* [2002] 2 All ER 1. In general, the HSE's approach appears to ignore some of the difficulties identified by the Court of Appeal, such as the multiple causes of stress, the difficulties that employers may have in knowing how their employees are likely to react to various factors and the difficulties in implementing appropriate control measures once the problem has been identified. The HSE recognises that stress is a difficult management issue within the workplace, but nevertheless advocates that employers take a proactive approach. The risk assessment should be the starting point to determine what further action employers can take.

5.3 RISK ASSESSMENT

The terminology used in the concept of risk assessment is defined in the Approved Code of Practice for the Management of Health and Safety at Work Regulations, as follows:

1. A hazard is something with the potential to cause harm.
2. A risk is the likelihood of potential harm from that hazard being realised.
3. The extent of risk will depend on:

   (a) the likelihood of the harm occurring;
   (b) the potential severity of that harm (resultant injury or adverse ill health effect); and
   (c) the number of people who might be affected by the hazard or exposed to it.

The process of risk assessment requires employers to carry out five steps.

Step 1: Identify the hazards

The first step is to identify the relevant hazards. In the context of workplace stress, the hazards will take the form of work-related stress stressors, of which the best known are:

- poorly designed/managed workload;
- poorly designed/managed work scheduling;
- poorly designed/managed work design;
- poorly designed/managed physical environment;
- lack of skill discretion/control;
- lack of decision authority/control;
- lack of appropriate pro-active support;
- lack of appropriate reactive support;
- poorly designed or managed procedures for eliminating conflict at individual/team level (including bullying/harassment).

There may be other stressors that may be relevant to particular employers. For example, employers who are planning or undergoing a period of change (e.g. downsizing) may find that the managerial and operational decisions accompanying the relevant changes are a significant cause of stress to their employees. Cultural issues, such as a lack of communication and consultation within the organisation or an expectation that employees will conform to certain behavioural norms (e.g. the long hours culture or a 'macho' culture), can also be significant sources of workplace stress.

Step 2: Decide who is at risk

The second stage of the risk assessment process is to consider who might be harmed by these particular stressors and how. Some stressors may affect the workforce in general and this is particularly likely to be true of physical and environmental stressors. Others may only affect particular sections of the workforce. For example, a particular department or team may have a significantly greater workload than other parts of the undertaking. Similarly, a particular department or team may be reorganised or downsized and employees in that department may therefore be exposed to greater levels of stress than others in the same organisation.

It may even be the case that particular individuals are known to be more likely to be harmed by particular stressors than others, such as any employee who has already, to the employer's knowledge, suffered a psychiatric condition or reaction to particular workplace stressors. The Management of Health and Safety at Work Regulations requires specific attention to be paid to young employees and new or expectant mothers, as these groups may react to stressors differently from the general working population. This should be reflected in this stage of the risk assessment.

Step 3: Evaluate the risk

The third stage is for the employer to evaluate the risks (i.e. the likelihood that potential harm will follow from exposure to the hazards identified in the first step). It is clear that the HSE does not interpret likelihood of harm in this context in the same way as foreseeability in the context of negligence (see **Chapters 2** and **3**). Although there may be individuals in relation to whom known personal factors will make the likelihood of harm greater than to employees in general, it is clear that the HSE considers that workplace stress is something which could cause harm to employees at large – a principle that was expressly rejected by the Court of Appeal when it considered the concept of foreseeability in claims based on negligence.

The evaluation of risks is likely to be the most difficult stage of the risk assessment. Whether such a generalised approach can be borne out by the available scientific evidence is questionable. The HSE recently commissioned research by the Institute of Employment Studies to identify the available evidence on the ways in which the stress as listed above could affect individuals at work. (*Review of Existing Supporting Scientific Knowledge to Underpin Standards of Good Practice to Key Work Related Stressors – Phase 1, 2002.*) The review covered the available evidence on the impact of work-related stress on both employees' performance and their health.

The research concluded that the available evidence was, at best, mixed. In the case of poorly managed workloads, for example, a mixed pattern of relationships was found. Some of the available evidence suggested that increases in workload had a negative impact on individuals, whilst other evidence pointed towards low work rates having the same effect. However, a number of studies found that there was evidence that there was a relationship between workloads and an individual's health and well-being. In the case of work design, the available evidence was very limited, but that which there was suggested that changes to work design might lead to improvements in work-related performance, but not necessarily to mental health. On the other hand, a lack of support from management or appropriate training was generally found to have a negative impact on both work-related and health-related outcomes.

The patchy nature of the evidence suggests that employers may face difficulties when carrying out their risk assessments. In the absence of anything specific to suggest that a particular individual is likely to be at risk (such as complaints about health from the employee or knowledge of a pre-existing condition), there is simply insufficient evidence to allow the employer to infer that individuals will all react in the same way to workplace stressors.

To assist employers, the HSE intends to publish management standards (see below), although how effective and/or universally applicable those will in fact be is questionable, bearing in mind the unsatisfactory state of the scientific evidence used to underpin and formulate the standards.

Step 4: Record the findings

The fourth stage ought to be to record the findings of the risk assessment. This is only a mandatory requirement for employers who have five or more employees, but would clearly be good practice in the case of most employers, not least because it may be difficult to recall and review the steps deemed necessary in light of the risk assessment if they are not recorded anywhere.

Step 5: Implementation and review

The final step is to implement the findings and review them regularly. The implementation process should also consider the effectiveness of the identified precautions. This involves, first, checking whether the intended precaution is actually being taken in the workplace and, secondly, whether this precaution is achieving the desired result or whether it needs some form of modification.

It is an express requirement that the risk assessment should be reviewed, first, when there is reason to suspect it is no longer valid and, secondly, when there has been a significant change to the matters to which it relates. In practice, risk assessments need to be reviewed periodically, in light of any accident or other unforeseen event which shows that the original risk assessment is no longer appropriate and at any time that there is a significant change in the way that the organisation conducts itself. This may due to the implementation of new procedures, the employment of new personnel, the development of a new product or a change in premises.

Similar considerations to those set out above will apply where workplace stress is being considered as a factor which increases the risk posed by other workplace hazards. An employee who is experienced in high levels of workplace stress may react differently to exposure to such other hazards, compared with one who is not experiencing unnecessary levels of stress. A simple example of the types of hazard where an employee's reaction to stress may be relevant is the physical or environmental surroundings in which the employee works. Issues such as noise, lighting or ventilation may affect an employee who is already experiencing excessive levels of stress to a greater degree. Where appropriate, employers should aim to demonstrate that excessive levels of stress have been considered as a factor increasing risk in the risk assessments for the other workplace hazards.

5.4 THE HSE'S PROPOSED MANAGEMENT STANDARDS

The HSE has identified the management and reduction of workplace stress as one of its priority programmes until 2007. In addition, a challenging target has been set to secure a 20 per cent reduction in work-related ill health over that period and a 30 per cent reduction in work days lost due to ill health. Further, there is a growing recognition of the need to rehabilitate individuals who have suffered work-related ill health into the workforce.

An important part of these initiatives as far as the HSE is concerned is the implementation of a set of management standards for the control of workplace stress. The HSE recognises that these standards must be based on evidence and is also aware of the need to ensure that the standards are:

- practical and easy to use;
- of general application;
- focused on the problems posed by workplace stress and their solutions;
- flexible and adaptable to many different workplace needs;
- supported by a business case.

As indicated above, the proposed management standards may hit a fundamental stumbling block because of the lack of supporting evidence. In the case of the extent to which an individual employee has control over his job, for example, the available evidence suggests that a low level of control has a negative impact on work-related performance, but was more mixed in terms of the impact on health. Developing a set of standards which are intended to have widespread applicability in this area may, therefore, be very difficult because the evidence that any particular steps will improve the health of employees is simply unavailable.

5.5 ENFORCEMENT

As indicated above, the HSE has tended, to date, to tread softly on the question of enforcement action against employers who fail to discharge the duty to manage workplace stress. In theory, however, a number of enforcement options are available for both contraventions of the Health and Safety at Work etc. Act 1974 and any associated regulations.

Improvement notices

An improvement notice may be served if an HSE inspector is of the opinion that a person is contravening one or more of the relevant statutory provisions or has contravened one or more of these provisions in circumstances that make it likely that the contravention will continue or be repeated.

The improvement notice must state that the inspector is of the opinion summarised above, must specify the provisions which have in his opinion been contravened, must give particulars for the reasons for the opinion and must specify a period of time within which the contravention must be remedied.

The period specified in the notice must be at least 21 days, this being the period allowed for an appeal against the service of an improvement notice. The appeal lies to the Employment Tribunal and the effect of lodging an appeal is to suspend the requirements of the improvement notice until the appeal has been determined.

There were formerly provisions which required the HSE inspector to give notice of his intention to serve an improvement notice and, although the provisions have been withdrawn, it is good practice for inspectors to consult employers before serving such a notice.

Any failure to comply with the improvement notice is a criminal offence, punishable by either a fine or imprisonment.

Prohibition notices

There may be occasions where the activities carried out by an employer are such that they involve or may involve a risk of serious personal injury. In such cases, the appropriate step is for the inspector to serve a prohibition notice. It is difficult to contemplate the circumstances in which this might be appropriate in the case of activities which expose employees to workplace stress, simply because there is no generally accepted level at which such activities will pose a risk of harm to health.

In the event that an inspector considers that a prohibition notice is appropriate, the consequence for the employer may be that the activity in question has to be ceased immediately. Whilst there is a right of appeal to the Employment Tribunal, the exercise of this right will not suspend the operation of the prohibition notice, in contrast to the improvement notice referred to above.

Investigation of suspected health and safety breaches

Inspectors have very wide powers to investigate any potential breaches of the health and safety legislation. A comprehensive list is set out under s.20 of the Health and Safety at Work etc. Act 1974. Relevant powers in the context of breaches in relation to workplace stress include the power to:

- enter and search premises;
- interview any person;
- require the production and inspection of any documents and take copies;
- require the provision of facilities and assistance for the purpose of carrying out the investigation.

When exercising their s.20 powers, inspectors have the right to require interviewees to answer such questions as they think fit to ask and to sign a declaration that those answers are true.

There is some anecdotal evidence of inspectors responding by exercising their investigative powers where they receive complaints of high levels of workplace stress (e.g. at Wolverhampton University in 2002) and it may be that the mere threat of such an investigation will be sufficient to compel the employer in question to take action to correct the breaches.

Prosecutions

If the inspector is satisfied that an employer is in breach of its duty to manage stress in the workplace, then it is open to the inspector to bring a prosecution against the employer in question. In the context of workplace stress, this could either be under the general duty in the Health and Safety at Work etc. Act 1974, or for a breach of the requirement to carry out a risk assessment. These breaches are 'either way' offences, exposing the employer to a fine of up to £20,000 in the Magistrates' Court and an unlimited fine in the Crown Court.

In relation to charges under the Act, the main defence available to employers is to show that they have taken all actions which were reasonably practicable to prevent harm to the health, safety and welfare of employees. The defence of reasonable practicability enables employers to set-off the costs of implementing control measures against the benefits that are anticipated from those control measures. Potentially, this could be a useful defence for employers facing charges in relation to the failure to manage workplace stress, particularly where the available scientific evidence does not support a link between exposure to workplace stress and harm to health.

In relation to risk assessments, it remains more likely in the foreseeable future that charges will relate to a failure to carry out an assessment of the risks posed by stressors in the workplace, rather than a challenge to the suitability or sufficiency of the assessment. If, however, the proposed management standards are implemented by the HSE, then these could be used as a benchmark for the type of action that the reasonable employer will be expected to take in the future.

Whatever defence the employer seeks to run, the onus is on the employer to satisfy the court on the balance of probabilities that the defence should apply. It is for the prosecution to then prove beyond reasonable doubt that the employer should not be entitled to avail itself of the defence, because, for example, there were other steps that were reasonably practicable for the employer to take, which it failed to take.

5.6 CIVIL LIABILITY

Neither the Health and Safety at Work etc. Act 1974 nor the Management of Health and Safety at Work Regulations confers a right of civil action by an employee who has suffered loss or damage because of an employer's failure to comply with the duties imposed. Both, however, can be relied on as evidence of negligence: a negligent failure to have regard to the regulations may therefore be a relevant factor. In addition, it is intended to remove the civil liability exclusion from the regulations in the near future and this could be a fruitful area for employees who have developed psychiatric injuries and whose employers have taken no steps to comply with the regulations.

5.7 PRACTICAL CONSIDERATIONS

For most employers, the sequence for dealing with the health and safety aspects of workplace stress is likely to be as follows:

1. Identify whether excessive levels of stress are a hazard present in their particular workplace (gathering and analysing the available evidence through an audit or a survey of employees).
2. Assess the risk posed by the workplace stressors identified in the audit or survey (the risk assessment).
3. Implement appropriate control measures (developing a stress management strategy).

Identifying whether stress is a relevant issue

The starting point for an employer seeking to discharge its obligations under the health and safety at work legislation, in so far as those relate to workplace stress, will be to establish whether or not stress is a relevant workplace issue for its undertaking. This can either be done through a simple questionnaire, circulated amongst employees to establish whether or not they perceive workplace stress as a relevant occupational issue for them, or a more detailed stress audit carried out by external specialists. For most employers, it will be sensible to begin by making enquiries of their employees to ensure that any action taken is based on the actual circumstances prevailing in the workplace, rather than proceeding on the basis of assumptions or unspecified perceptions which may be based on limited and not necessarily reliable evidence, such as complaints actually made by employees.

It is important to the success of this process that employees are reassured as to why the information is sought. There is an understandable reluctance amongst employees to disclose to their employer that they are struggling, either with their workload, or with factors such as their relationship with their managers. Employees ought to be asked to identify aspects of their employment which they find particularly positive or negative. There is an obvious need to have gained their trust so that they will be able to provide completely honest answers to the enquiries without facing any form of reprisals, if the information provided by them is to be relied upon.

The following checklists may assist in deciding to proceed with the stress audit.

Before the audit

1. Explain to staff about the process which is to be undertaken and its purposes.
2. Assess what level of enquiries need to be made. For example, an employer who already has numerous employees absent with stress-related illnesses may need to make more detailed enquiries than an employer who has yet to receive significant complaints about the problems.
3. Identify how the responses are to be assessed: is this something that the employer can carry out in-house, or will specialist expertise be needed?

During the audit

4. Ensure that any employees who have any concerns about the audit have someone with whom they can discuss their concerns about completing the questionnaire.
5. Ensure that the process of gathering the information does not become stressful in itself for employees.
6. Ensure that managers understand why the information is being sought and that it will not be used to target particular individuals with management functions where complaints are directed specifically at them.

After the audit

7. Ensure that employees are aware of what the information will be used for, including the time frame within which any action will be taken.

8. Involve staff and/or representatives in the process of determining what action should be taken following the audit.
9. Review any action taken as a result of the audit to ensure it is achieving the desired result.

The stress audit will enable an employer to determine whether or not there is a problem with workplace stress in its undertaking. If excessive levels of workplace stress are identified as a workplace factor, then these should be treated as a workplace hazard which requires a more formal risk assessment carried out, in line with the principles outlined above.

Developing a stress management policy

Once the risk assessment is completed, one of the measures which may be identified as needed to decrease the risks posed by workplace stress is to develop a stress management policy. The aim of the stress management policy should be to set out for employees and any other external bodies that may have an interest in reviewing the same (e.g. the HSE) what the employer has done to tackle stress as a workplace issue in its undertaking. It is also an opportunity for the employer to ensure that employees understand their own responsibilities if they feel that they are experiencing excessive levels of workplace stress.

The policy should set out the support that will be offered to employees who consider that they are experiencing excessive levels of workplace stress, including policies for referral to occupational health (if available) or access to counselling schemes. There should be a provision in the policy for ongoing monitoring of the problem, including review of the policy itself and a mechanism for providing information and training to employees on stress-related issues, such as how to identify and recognise symptoms of stress in themselves or in colleagues and understanding the measures that the employer has implemented to manage or reduce occupational stress.

5.8 CONCLUSION

It will be readily apparent that the approach advocated by the HSE is fundamentally different from the tests applied by the Court of Appeal in line with the guidelines in *Sutherland* v. *Hatton* (see **Chapter 3**). The overall effect of the guidelines in *Hatton* is that, in most cases, employers will be entitled to adopt a reactive approach to stress as a workplace issue. For example, they will be entitled to wait until an employee advises them that he has a problem as a result of stress in the workplace, they will be entitled to expect the employee and/or his medical advisers to take a leading role in identifying what action the employee wishes to see taken as a result of the symptoms experienced and they may be able to evade all liability by providing, for example, access to a relevant counselling service.

By way of contrast, the HSE has made it clear that access to counselling services is not, in its view, an appropriate approach to stress management, although it may have a valuable role to play as part of a wider package of measures implemented by the employer. On the face of it, the HSE's approach appears more logical. If an employee's problems are caused by the nature of the work he is being asked to do, by workload or by his relationship with managers, then it is difficult to see how counselling alone will resolve those and prevent any aggravation in a known condition or deterioration in the employee's health, as, presumably, the employee will be returned to the very conditions that are causing the problem at the conclusion of every counselling session.

Whilst it may be tempting for employers to favour the Court of Appeal's approach, there is much to be said in favour of adopting a proactive approach to stress management. First, it will enable employers and employees to identify problems at an early stage, when finding a solution may be easier. Secondly, an employer who has shown itself to be receptive to the problems posed by stress will have more of a defence to any claim by an employee that he has been made ill by his work if that employee has not raised significant problems with stress at an early stage. Finally, a proper stress management strategy will enable the employer to take a robust approach to spurious claims by employees in relation to workplace stress. For example, it is now increasingly the case that employees who are to be disciplined fail to attend the disciplinary hearing on grounds of stress, or seek to mount a collateral challenge to the employer's decision to take disciplinary action by claiming they have been subjected to excessive levels of stress. If the employer has in place a sensible stress management policy, then it may enable the employer to proceed with the disciplinary action, with less need to fear that the action will be the subject of later challenge through the courts or the tribunals.

CHAPTER 6

Disability discrimination

6.1 INTRODUCTION

Employees suffering from stress and stress-related illnesses are increasingly likely to bring claims in the Employment Tribunals, alleging discrimination under the Disability Discrimination Act 1995 ('the DDA').

This is the case whether the stress is caused by a work-related factor, such as bullying, harassment or long hours, or whether its cause is unrelated to the workplace, such as family or relationship problems. Unlike the situation under the law of negligence and health and safety, the DDA is not concerned with the cause of the disability, it is the fact that an employee or potential employee is disabled that could give rise to liability. For this reason, the DDA's practical implications are potentially very broad and it can offer employees wider protection than that offered by other types of claims.

However, establishing disability discrimination can prove to be difficult in practice. Essentially it involves four key questions (see *Clark* v. *TDG Limited t/a Novacold* [1999] IRLR 318, CA):

1. Is the employee disabled?
2. Is the employee being treated less favourably for a reason related to that disability?
3. Are any reasonable adjustments necessary to accommodate the employee?
4. Is the proposed course of action in relation to the employee capable of being justified?

Each of these questions needs to be examined in detail and whether or not a particular applicant can get over the various thresholds imposed by the DDA depends on difficult issues of fact and degree.

6.2 ESTABLISHING DISABILITY

The first, and often the most difficult, issue to be established by an employee is that he satisfies the definition of a disabled person under the DDA. This issue is often decided by an Employment Tribunal at a preliminary hearing, rather than at the hearing of the substantive claim and, although tribunals tend to take a more inquisitorial and interventionist role in DDA claims than they do in some other types of cases, many claims fail at this first hurdle.

Section 1(1) of the DDA defines disability as 'a physical or mental impairment which has a substantial and long-term adverse effect on [the person's] ability to carry out normal day-to-day activities'.

The onus is on the individual to establish, on the balance of probabilities, that he satisfied this definition as at the relevant date, i.e. the date of the alleged discriminatory act rather than the date of the Employment Tribunal hearing (see *Cruickshank* v. *VAW Motorcast Limited* [2002] IRLR 24, EAT). This will involve detailed evidence from the individual about his condition and, in most cases, medical evidence will also be necessary.

There are four elements of the definition and each of these elements needs to be established in order for an individual to be afforded protection under the DDA.

Physical or mental impairment

When dealing with stress-related claims, a stress-related illness may, in itself, amount to an impairment, but it is also important to recognise that stress may aggravate other conditions to the extent that these conditions become impairments. Therefore, although individuals making stress-related disability claims are most likely to claim that they are suffering from a mental impairment, there is also the possibility of claims in respect of physical impairments, such as irritable bowel syndrome or migraine.

In the case of a mental impairment, the individual will have to show that the impairment results from or consists of a mental illness, which is a clinically well-recognised illness (see DDA, Sched.1, para.1). This can be difficult to establish in practice.

It is important to note that stress, in itself, is not a mental impairment, although it may be a factor contributing to an impairment. Stress-related illnesses may be mental impairments, depending on the circumstances. Examples of mental illnesses that may amount to mental impairments are reactive depression and chronic fatigue syndrome.

The Employment Appeal Tribunal in the case of *Morgan* v. *Staffordshire University* [2002] IRLR 190 provided practical guidance on the type of evidence required to prove that an individual is suffering from a mental impairment.

In this case, the evidence before the Employment Tribunal consisted of general practitioners' sickness certificates referring to 'anxiety', 'stress', 'nervous debility' and 'depression'. This evidence was held to be insufficient, without further explanation, to establish that Mrs Morgan was suffering from a clinically well-recognised mental illness.

The EAT held that the issue of whether or not an individual was suffering from a mental impairment was a matter for qualified and informed medical opinion. Although a full consultant psychiatrist's report is not always necessary, and often a general practitioner's letter will suffice, the tribunal will need more than vague and loose terms, such as those contained in Mrs Morgan's sickness certificates, to make a finding that the employee is suffering from a mental impairment. The EAT stressed that, in disability claims, the parties should not expect the tribunal to have more than a layman's rudimentary familiarity with psychiatric classification. A sustainable medical diagnosis is essential.

Establishing a mental impairment requires:

- proof of a mental illness mentioned in the World Health Organisation's International Classification of Diseases;
- proof of a mental illness specifically mentioned in a similar publication; or
- proof by other means of a medical illness recognised by a respected body of medical opinion.

Establishing the existence of either a physical or a mental impairment will, therefore, largely depend on medical evidence. The burden of proof is on the individual to establish the existence of an impairment and, in the absence of fairly detailed and specific medical evidence, it is unlikely that this burden will be discharged.

Ability to carry out normal day-to-day activities

When considering the effect that the impairment has on an individual's ability to carry out normal day-to-day activities, Employment

Tribunals have to look at a number of physical and mental attributes (see DDA, Sched.1, para.4).

The impairment must affect one of the following:

- mobility;
- manual dexterity;
- physical co-ordination;
- continence;
- ability to lift, carry or otherwise move everyday objects;
- speech, hearing or eyesight;
- memory or ability to learn, concentrate or understand; or
- perception of the risk of physical danger.

In stress-related claims, although mental attributes such as memory and ability to concentrate, learn and understand are usually going to be the most relevant, it is also worth bearing in mind that the tiredness and fatigue associated with some mental illnesses may affect physical attributes, such as mobility and manual dexterity, particularly as regards a person's ability to sustain these activities over a reasonable period of time. With mental illnesses, it may also be more difficult to point to the particular abilities that are affected than in cases which involve physical impairments.

The Employment Tribunals will look at what are considered to be normal day-to-day activities for most people, so these should be activities that are carried out by the majority of people on a daily or frequent and fairly regular basis. Employment Tribunals should not be concerned with the normal activities of a particular individual or the particular duties of a job.

The effect on day-to-day activities must be assessed in such a way that if an impairment would have a substantial effect but for the fact that measures are being taken to treat or correct it, it is to be treated as having that effect (see DDA, Sched.1, para.6). The measures referred to in the DDA specifically include medical treatment, but what constitutes medical treatment has been a matter of some debate.

In the case of *Kapadia* v. *London Borough of Lambeth* [2001] IRLR 14, the Employment Appeal Tribunal was concerned with the issue of whether an employee's impairment should be assessed before or after taking into account the counselling he was receiving for his illness.

Mr Kapadia suffered from stress, anxiety and depression and was diagnosed with reactive depression. This affected his ability to concentrate. He was referred to a clinical psychologist for counselling sessions. There was evidence before the Employment Tribunal that, without the counselling he was receiving, there was a strong likelihood that Mr Kapadia would have had a total mental breakdown and would have needed in-patient psychiatric treatment.

The EAT held that, in determining whether the impairment had a substantial effect on Mr Kapadia's ability to carry out normal day-to-day activities, it was necessary to consider what the effect would have been but for the treatment he was receiving by way of counselling.

The same principle applies when an individual is on medication for his illness, e.g. anti-depressants. The Employment Tribunal has to look at how the individual's abilities were actually affected at the relevant time whilst taking the medication and it will then have to try to establish what it believes the effects would have been without the medication, i.e. the deduced effects. Medical evidence on this point will be needed to assist the Employment Tribunal in making its assessment.

There are some treatments that it is hoped will bring about a permanent improvement in the individual's impairment. However, the fact that such an improvement may occur should be disregarded until it is clear whether or not the permanent improvement has, in fact, occurred and until then the effect of the treatment should be disregarded in assessing the impairment (see *Abadeh* v. *British Telecommunications plc* [2001] IRLR 23, EAT).

Substantial effect

Whether an effect is substantial is the ingredient of the definition of disability that often generates the most difficulty in practice. Substantial in this context means more than minor or trivial.

In determining whether the effect is substantial, the Employment Tribunal will have to make an overall assessment based on the evidence and the Employment Appeal Tribunal in the case of *Leonard* v. *Southern Derbyshire Chamber of Commerce* [2001] IRLR 19 stressed the importance of this.

Ms Leonard suffered from clinical depression. One of her symptoms was that she tired very easily, affecting her mobility, manual dexterity, physical co-ordination and ability to concentrate. In considering whether her impairment had a substantial adverse effect on her ability to carry out normal day-to-day activities, the Employment Tribunal found that Ms Leonard could catch a ball, but tripped over pavement edges; she could thread a needle, but could not maintain sufficient concentration to sew; she could remember the names of her children and her work colleagues, but could not remember everything that happened from day-to-day. The Employment Tribunal weighed up the evidence and concluded that there was no substantial adverse effect on Ms Leonard's ability to carry out normal day-to-day activities.

The Employment Appeal Tribunal overturned the decision, stressing that the focus should be on what the employee cannot do, rather than on what the employee can do. This is a trap which is easily fallen into. Just because an employee can do certain things perfectly well does not mean that he is not substantially impaired from doing other things that persons without the impairment would take for granted.

In *Goodwin* v. *The Patent Office* [1999] IRLR 4, the Employment Appeal Tribunal stressed that it is important to consider the adjustments that disabled people often make to their lives and circumstances to enable them to cope.

Mr Goodwin was a paranoid schizophrenic, who suffered from thought broadcasting whereby he imagined that other people could read his thoughts and he would misinterpret the words and actions of colleagues in a paranoid fashion. He also had auditory hallucinations and found it difficult to concentrate for sustained periods. However, he was able to perform domestic tasks without assistance, get to work efficiently and carry out his work satisfactorily.

In determining whether his impairment had a substantial adverse effect on his ability to carry out normal day-to-day activities, the EAT said that just because Mr Goodwin was able to cope at home did not mean that he was not disabled.

The EAT said that it was necessary to look not only at the things a person cannot do, but also at the things he can only do with difficulty. Just because an individual can carry out a certain activity does not mean that his ability to do so is not impaired. The emphasis should be on the individual's ability to do or not to do an activity, rather than on the actual doing of the act.

It should also be borne in mind that disabled people often develop coping strategies in their daily lives and may have a tendency to 'play down' the effects of their disability. The message is that appearances can deceive, so a proper analysis of all impairments is required to ascertain whether, in fact, they have a substantial adverse effect.

Long-term effect

Under Sched.1, para.2 to the DDA, the effect of an impairment will be long-term if:

- it has lasted or is expected to last for at least 12 months;
- it is likely to last for the rest of the life of the person affected; or
- it is likely to recur.

When assessing whether the effect of an impairment is likely to last for 12 months, it is necessary to take into account the total period for which the effect exists, both before and after the date of the discrimination. This means that the Employment Tribunal will consider adverse effects up to and including the hearing, and not just up to the date of the allegedly discriminatory act (see *Greenwood* v. *British Airways plc* [1999] IRLR 600, EAT).

The question of whether or not an individual is disabled is ultimately one for the Employment Tribunal, based on an assessment of the particular circumstances, and it can involve difficult questions of fact and degree and an assessment of detailed medical evidence.

When dealing with any impairment, whether physical or mental, it is not the particular condition that is important but the effect it has. Therefore, from a practical point of view, in many cases the Employment Tribunal will need more than just a description of the impairment, but will need to know when and how it manifests itself and medical evidence is usually crucial.

The role of medical reports is:

- to provide a diagnosis of the impairment;
- to provide observations on the individual's ability to carry out normal day-to-day activities;
- to provide a likely prognosis;
- to estimate the effects of any treatment.

Before going to the expense of obtaining detailed medical reports, the parties in a DDA claim should consider whether some agreement can be reached on the evidence available. It is also worth bearing in mind that, as with personal injury claims, Employment Tribunals are increasingly requiring the parties to instruct a single joint medical expert, rather than incurring the expense of two sets of experts' reports.

It is also important to note that, although medical evidence plays a significant role in most disability claims, the decision as to whether or not an individual is disabled is ultimately one for the Employment

Tribunal, based on all the evidence, and this decision-making process should not be delegated to medical experts (see *Abadeh* v. *British Telecommunications plc* [2001] IRLR 23, EAT and *Vicary* v. *British Telecommunications plc* [1999] IRLR 680, EAT).

6.3 ESTABLISHING DISCRIMINATION

Once an individual has established that he is a disabled person within the meaning of the DDA, he then has to show that he has been discriminated against for a reason related to that disability.

Discrimination can take one of three forms:

- less favourable treatment;
- failure to make reasonable adjustments; or
- victimisation.

Discrimination can occur both during employment, including the terms and conditions upon which an employee is employed, and during the recruitment process, including determining who should be offered employment and on what terms. The House of Lords has recently confirmed that the DDA also protects individuals against discrimination or victimisation that occurs after the employment relationship has ended (see *Relaxia Group plc* v. *Rhys-Harper and other cases* [2003] UKHL 33).

From a practical point of view, stress-related illnesses are most likely to be an issue, either when deciding whether or not to recruit a potential employee who has a history of mental illness, or where an existing employee becomes disabled due to a stress-related illness and the employer has to decide how to deal with the situation.

Discrimination may arise in any of the following areas:

- recruitment;
- job offers;
- terms and conditions of employment;
- salary and benefits;
- training;
- promotion;
- redundancy;
- dismissal; or
- retirement.

Less favourable treatment

Discrimination occurs under s.5(1) of the DDA when, for a reason which relates to a person's disability, an employer treats him less favourably than it treats or would treat others to whom that reason does not or would not apply.

In *Clark* v. *TDG Limited t/a Novacold* [1999] IRLR 318, the Court of Appeal made it clear that the comparison should be with someone who does not suffer from the adverse effects of the disability and that assessing whether there has been less favourable treatment involves a three-stage process:

1. the reason for the treatment should be identified;
2. it then has to be decided whether that reason relates to the person's disability; and
3. finally, there needs to be a comparison between the treatment of the disabled employee and the way in which the employer would treat a person to whom the reason for the treatment did not apply.

If less favourable treatment has occurred, then the key issue will be justification.

Where an employer is concerned with an employee who is absent from work on long-term sick leave due to a stress-related disability, the disabled employee should be compared not with an employee who is absent from work for the same period of time for a reason other than a disability, but to a person who is not absent from work, i.e. someone who is not suffering from the adverse effects of the disability, in this case the inability to attend work and perform the job.

The practical effect of this is that, if an employer dismisses a disabled employee who has been absent from work for a period of time due to a disability on the grounds of his absence, it will be discriminating against him. The question will then be whether the discrimination is capable of being justified.

Whether or not an employer has to have knowledge of the disability, or at least the material features of it, in order to treat an individual less favourably has been a matter of some debate. Originally, the case law proceeded on the basis that knowledge or imputed knowledge of a disability was necessary (see *O'Neill* v. *Symm* [1998] IRLR 233, EAT*)*, but, more recently, the case law has moved away from this concept and it has become clearer that knowledge of a disability is unnecessary and that the test should be an objective one of whether there is a relationship between the reason for the treatment and the individual's disability (see *H J Heinz Co Limited* v. *Kenrick* [2000] IRLR 144, EAT and *London Borough of Hammersmith & Fulham* v. *Farnsworth* [2000] IRLR 691, EAT). The employer's state of knowledge will, however, often be highly material to the question of whether or not the less favourable treatment is justified.

Although the decisions are conflicting on this issue, the only practical advice for employers is to assume that discrimination can occur not only where they have knowledge of the disability, but also where they do not. Ignorance of a disability will probably not help an employer if it discriminates for a reason related to that disability, so proper consideration and examination of all medical conditions is essential.

Failure to make reasonable adjustments

The second form of discrimination under the DDA is a failure to make reasonable adjustments under s.5(2).

Discrimination occurs if arrangements made by the employer or physical features of the premises occupied by the employer place a disabled person at a substantial disadvantage in comparison with non-disabled persons and the employer does not take such steps as it is reasonable for it to take, in all the circumstances to prevent the arrangements or features having that effect (see DDA, s.6(1)).

In the case of *Morse* v. *Wiltshire County Council* [1998] IRLR 352, the EAT set out the sequential steps for establishing whether there has been a failure to make a reasonable adjustment:

1. Is there a duty imposed on the employer to make reasonable adjustments in this particular case?
2. Has the employer taken such steps as are reasonable in all the circumstances for it to have to take in order to comply with its duty?
3. If not, is the failure to comply with the duty justified?

When assessing what adjustments are reasonable, the Employment Tribunal should take into account issues such as effectiveness, practicability, financial and other costs, the extent of any disruption, the employer's financial and other resources and the availability of financial and other assistance (see DDA, s.6(4)).

It is for the employer to explore what reasonable adjustments may be appropriate in the circumstances and not necessarily for the employee to suggest what adjustments may be necessary.

Examples of possible reasonable adjustments include:

- moving the individual to a less stressful position;
- allocating some duties to another employee;
- altering working hours;
- providing additional assistance;
- allowing absences for treatment;
- providing counselling.

The state of the employer's knowledge of a disability is relevant to the issue of reasonable adjustments, as no duty arises to make such adjustments if the employer does not know and could not reasonably be expected to know that the employee has a disability (see DDA, s.6(6)).

However, an employer's ignorance of the duty to make reasonable adjustments will not necessarily mean it will be in breach of its duty to make such adjustments. The issue is whether it has taken steps that are reasonable in the circumstances and this relates to what the employer did or did not do, and not what it considered. Therefore, there is nothing to prevent an employer from arguing after the event that it did not consider a particular step, but nevertheless it was not a reasonable one to take (see *British Gas Services Limited* v. *McCaull* [2001] IRLR 60, EAT). However, this may cause evidential difficulties.

Victimisation

The final form of discrimination is where a person is victimised for having brought proceedings under the DDA, given evidence or information in such proceedings, done anything under the DDA or made an allegation that another person has breached the DDA. Protection is also available where a person is victimised based on a belief or suspicion by another that he has done or intends to do any of these acts (see DDA, s.55).

6.4 JUSTIFICATION

If an employer treats a disabled person less favourably or if it fails to make reasonable adjustments to the individual's working arrangements, it will be discriminating against him. However, that is not the end of the story; the Employment Tribunal will then go on to consider whether the discrimination was justified (see DDA, ss.5(1)(b) and 5(2)(b)).

The reason for the justification must be both material to the circumstances of the particular case and substantial. Further, where discrimination takes the form of less favourable treatment, that treatment cannot be justified if there is a duty to make a reasonable adjustment and the employer fails, without justification, to make that adjustment (see DDA, s.5(5)).

The burden of establishing the defence of justification is on the employer and it must be a good business reason, and not one based on generalised or stereotypical assumptions. It is usually a balancing exercise between the interests of the employer and the employee.

As previously explained, an employer's knowledge of a disability will probably not be necessary to establish discrimination in claims of less favourable treatment, so, in such claims, the justification defence will be of critical importance. As justification depends on the way the employer treats the employee, knowledge of a disability is not necessarily an essential element, but the fact that the employer does not know that the disability exists may mean that the treatment is justified. What is required is a causal connection between the discriminatory act and the justifying circumstances (see *Callaghan* v. *Glasgow City Council* [2001] IRLR 724, EAT).

A practical example of when less favourable treatment may be justified is in the case of an employee on long-term sick leave due to a stress-related illness. If the employee is completely unable to carry out the main functions of his job, no reasonable adjustments can be made to his working arrangements to accommodate him and his absence is likely to continue for a significant period, the employer may well be justified in dismissing him. However, before doing so, it should obtain and consider medical evidence of the employee's condition and consult with the employee to ensure that there are no adjustments that could be made to facilitate his return to work, whether to his original role or to some other vacant post.

If an employer fails to consider its duty to make reasonable adjustments, through ignorance of the duty, then, again, state of knowledge may be relevant when it comes to justification. If an employer is ignorant of the extent of the disability and its effects then it may be able to justify any failure to make reasonable adjustments (see *Wright* v. *Governors of Bilton High School and Warwickshire County Council*, EAT, 12 April 2002). However, each case will turn on its own facts and an employer should not bury its head in the sand in the hope of then being able to rely on its ignorance to justify its failure to act.

6.5 THE CONSEQUENCES OF DISCRIMINATION

A disabled person can bring a claim in the Employment Tribunals in respect of an employer's discrimination under the DDA. Such a claim must be brought within three months of the act complained of or within such further time as the Employment Tribunal considers just and equitable in all the circumstances.

An Employment Tribunal can make a declaration of rights, can make a recommendation as to specific actions and it can order the employer to pay potentially unlimited compensation.

Compensation is made up of two parts:

1. An award for loss of earnings. Where an employee has been dismissed as a result of his disability, it may well be that there is a high award for future loss of earnings, as it is generally likely to take longer for a disabled person to find a job than someone who does not suffer from a disability. This is particularly the case with employees suffering from stress-related illnesses, where dismissal may exacerbate the illness or its effects.

2. An award for injury to feelings. The amount of such an award will depend on the seriousness of the case, with awards ranging from £500 for the least serious cases to around £25,000 for those that are most serious (see *Vento* v. *Chief Constable of West Yorkshire Police* [2003] IRLR 102, CA). This award can be increased if there are aggravating factors, so, if an employer dismisses an employee who is suffering from a stress-related illness and then unjustifiably adds to the employee's stress by strongly defending a claim which it has no prospect of winning, an Employment Tribunal may consider that a high award for injury to feelings is appropriate.

6.6 ESTABLISHING LIABILITY UNDER THE DISABILITY DISCRIMINATION ACT 1995

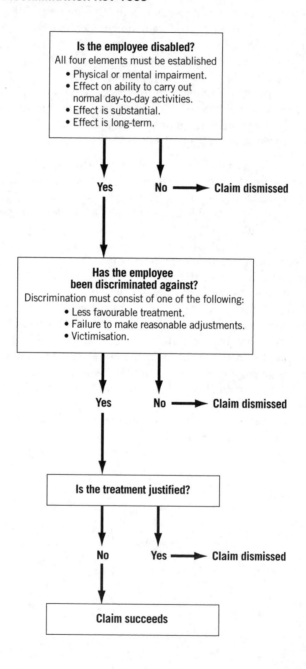

6.7 THE FUTURE

In May 2003 the draft Disability Discrimination Act 1995 (Amendment) Regulations 2003 (SI 2003/1673) were published, under which it is proposed to introduce some fairly wide-sweeping changes to disability discrimination law with effect from 1 October 2004. The changes include a refined definition of discrimination, an express prohibition on harassment and a tightening up of the rules on justification.

6.8 CONCLUSION

As liability under the DDA does not involve an employee having to prove that a stress-related illness was caused by the employer, DDA claims are used more frequently by employees suffering from work-related stress than negligence claims and disability discrimination claims often have better prospects of success.

However, vague descriptions of ailments such as 'stress' or 'debility' are not enough to establish that an employee is disabled: proof of a clinically well-recognised mental illness or a physical impairment is required. The employer may also be able to justify any discriminatory treatment.

From an employer's point of view, it should bear in mind that employees suffering from a stress-related illnesses might be disabled within the meaning of the DDA and that the actions it intends to take may amount to discrimination. The employer should try to keep itself well informed of the employee's medical condition and consult with the employee at every stage. Above all, it should be remembered that not every employee suffering from stress or a stress-related illness will be disabled, but, if in doubt, it is better to be overcautious than to risk a claim for potentially unlimited compensation.

CHAPTER 7

Bullying and harassment

7.1. INTRODUCTION

One of the major contributors to workplace stress and stress-related illnesses is bullying and harassment. It is estimated that between 8 and 10 per cent of employees within the EU are exposed to such conduct in the workplace and many victims of workplace bullying and harassment will suffer from stress-related illnesses as a result.

Over the last few years there have been several high-profile, high-value cases involving bullying at work and there has been a sharp increase in the number of stress claims, of a variety of different types, based on workplace bullying and harassment.

One of the factors contributing to this increase is undoubtedly the publicity that such cases often attract. However, the fact that it is now more difficult for negligence claims based on excessive workloads and long hours to succeed (see **Chapters 2** and **3**) may also be a reason why there is an increase in the number of stress-related claims based on bullying and harassment. After all, it would be difficult for an employer to argue that an employee voluntarily subjected himself to bullying and it may also be easier to identify the remedial steps that the employer could have taken to prevent or minimise the risk of bullying occurring.

A claim based on bullying and harassment may also, in certain circumstances, be preferable to a negligence claim from an employee's point of view, because it may allow the employee to recover compensation where he has not suffered from a recognised psychiatric disorder, but has nevertheless been distressed by his treatment.

In the UK, there is no specific legislation to deal with the issue of bullying and harassment in the workplace, so the victims of such behaviour currently have to rely on existing legal remedies that, because they were not designed for the purpose, are less than satisfactory. Nevertheless, workplace bullying and harassment can result in significant commercial and legal costs for an employer.

7.2 DEFINITION OF 'BULLYING'

There is currently no legal definition of 'bullying', but the most helpful working definition which has emerged is probably that of the Manufacturing Science and Finance Union (now Amicus):

> Persistent offensive, abusive, intimidating, malicious or insulting behaviour, abuse of power or unfair penal sanctions, which make the recipient feel upset, threatened, humiliated, or vulnerable, which undermines their self confidence and which may cause them to suffer stress.

Bullying often involves a misuse or abuse of power or authority and can be used to undermine the self-confidence of the victim. It often occurs between managers and their subordinates, but it can also arise between two employees on the same grade, or when a number of employees take action against one of their colleagues.

Bullying can take a variety of forms ranging from extreme physical violence to more subtle forms, such as making persistent negative comments or social isolation. It can consist of a series of minor incidents which may individually appear to be quite trivial, but the cumulative effect of which seriously undermines the employment relationship and can result in the employee suffering from a stress-related illness. Alternatively, it may take the form of a serious one-off incident.

Examples of bullying behaviour include:

- physical assault;
- threats, abuse or intimidation;
- offensive or abusive remarks;
- persistent negative comments;
- humiliating or belittling someone;
- unfair or excessive criticism;
- imposing excessive workloads or unattainable targets;
- making unnecessary demands;
- undervaluing work;
- claiming credit for someone else's work
- scape-goating;
- making false allegations;
- imposing unfair sanctions;
- ostracising someone.

7.3 DEFINITION OF 'HARASSMENT'

The term 'harassment' is often used colloquially to describe repetitious behaviour which is designed to wear someone down.

However, from a legal perspective, harassment is usually confined to behaviour based on the fact that the individual subjected to the harassment is protected by one or more of the discrimination statutes, i.e. the Sex Discrimination Act 1975 ('the SDA'), the Race Relations Act 1976 ('the RRA') or the Disability Discrimination Act 1995 ('the DDA').

It is not simply the unwelcome and unpleasant nature of the conduct which gives rise to potential liability, the victim has to show that he falls within one of the protected categories and that the harassment is on the grounds that he does so.

Like bullying, until recently there was no legal definition of 'harassment' and the definition adopted by the Employment Tribunals in reaching decisions in harassment cases was that set out in European Commission's Recommendation and Code of Practice on the Protection of the Dignity of Women and Men at Work (92/131/EEC):

> Unwanted conduct of a sexual nature or other conduct based on sex affecting the dignity of women and men at work. This can include unwelcome physical, verbal or non-verbal conduct.

The recommendation goes on to say that such conduct is unacceptable if it is unwanted, unreasonable and offensive to the recipient and it creates an intimidating, hostile or humiliating working environment.

With a little modification, this definition applied equally to racial harassment and harassment on the grounds of disability. For the immediate future this definition will continue to be used in connection with harassment on the grounds of sex.

From 19 July 2003 a statutory definition of harassment was, for the first time, introduced in the context of race discrimination by the Race Relations Act 1976 (Amendment) Regulations 2003 (SI 2003/1626):

> Unwanted conduct which has the purpose or effect of violating that other person's dignity, or creating an intimidating, hostile, degrading, humiliating or offensive environment for him.

This basic definition has been developed by case law, which has also set the parameters for the types of behaviour that may constitute harassment.

Unwanted conduct

One of the essential characteristics of harassment is that it is unwanted by the recipient. This means it must be unwelcome and uninvited.

It is for each individual to determine what behaviour is acceptable to him and what he regards as offensive. The test of whether the behaviour is unwanted is a subjective one and what one person regards as offensive, another may regard as normal social interaction.

In determining whether the individual actually found the behaviour offensive, evidence of his general attitude will be relevant in deciding whether, as a matter of fact, the behaviour was unwanted. For example, in a case of sexual harassment, evidence of the victim's general attitude to sexual behaviour may be relevant and admissible (see *Wileman* v. *Minilec Engineering Limited* [1988] IRLR 144, EAT and *Snowball* v. *Gardner Merchant Limited* [1987] IRLR 397, EAT).

One of the most contentious areas of harassment law is the issue of whether or not the individual has to expressly object to the conduct or whether objection can be implied from the circumstances.

The EU Code of Practice suggests that attention becomes harassment if it is persisted with once the recipient has made it clear that he regards it as offensive. However, the Code does recognise that one incident can constitute harassment if it is sufficiently serious.

On the other hand, case law recognises that it may be difficult for an employee to make a complaint about such conduct and that sometimes victims of harassment will suffer in silence, even though the conduct of the perpetrator is causing them significant distress (see *Wileman* v. *Minilec Engineering Limited* [1988] IRLR 144, EAT). Provided that a reasonable person would understand that the individual was rejecting the conduct complained of, continuation of the conduct would generally be regarded as harassment, so even expressing disapproval by walking out of a room may be sufficient (see *Reed & Bull Information Systems Limited* v. *Stedman* [1999] IRLR 299, EAT).

Examples of sexual harassment include:

- sexual assault;
- unwanted sexual contact;
- demeaning comments about a person's appearance;
- indecent remarks;
- leering;

- questions about a person's sex life;
- requests for sexual favours;
- name calling which is gender specific.

Course of conduct

Harassment is often used to describe a continuing course of conduct, but a one-off incident may constitute harassment if it is sufficiently serious. For example, in *Bracebridge Engineering Limited* v. *Darby* [1990] IRLR 3, the EAT held that a single incident of sexual assault was sufficiently serious to amount to sexual harassment and in *Insitu Cleaning Company Limited* v. *Heads* [1995] IRLR 4, the EAT held that one sexual remark was sufficient to amount to sexual harassment in the circumstances.

Whether or not a single act or a series of incidents amounts to harassment will be a question of fact and degree to be answered objectively by the Employment Tribunal in each particular set of circumstances.

When dealing with a course of conduct, the correct way of determining whether there has been harassment is not to take a fragmented approach, carving up the conduct into a series of incidents and deciding whether each incident is sufficiently serious to amount to harassment, but to look at all the circumstances and determine whether, in totality, the behaviour amounts to harassment. This should ensure that the cumulative effect of the behaviour is not diminished in determining whether it amounts to harassment (see *Reed & Bull Information Systems Limited* v. *Stedman* [1999] IRLR 299, EAT and *Qureshi* v. *Victoria University of Manchester* [2001] ICR 863, EAT).

Motive of the harasser

In order to constitute harassment, the motivation of the harasser may be taken into account, but an intention to harass the victim due to their protected status under one of the discrimination statutes is not an essential ingredient of harassment. Even if it can be shown that an employee not of the victim's sex, race or disability would have been treated equally unfavourably by the harasser, if the harassment is sex, race or disability specific then it will by contrary to the discrimination legislation (see *Strathclyde Regional Council* v. *Porcelli* [1986] IRLR 134, Court of Session).

7.4 THE COMMERCIAL AND PRACTICAL COSTS

Bullying and harassment can result in the victim suffering physical and/or psychological injury, including stress-related illnesses, which can lead to a variety of legal claims. However, it can also have a number of commercial and practical costs, which can have a wider effect on business than employers may at first expect, if it is allowed to continue.

Some of the consequences of bullying and harassment are:

- legal action;
- bad public image;
- reduced efficiency and productivity;
- reduced profitability;
- low staff morale;
- tension and conflict between colleagues;
- increased sickness absence;
- increased staff turnover;
- increased recruitment and training costs;
- increased likelihood of mistakes and accidents.

7.5 THE LEGAL CONSEQUENCES

At present, there is no one specific piece of legislation dealing with the issue of bullying and harassment in the workplace. The law on bullying and harassment at work is, in fact, a bit of a mess and often current legislation and legal principles have to be stretched to their limits in order to provide the victim of bullying and harassment with a remedy.

Assault

In extreme cases, bullying and harassment may amount to the common-law offences of assault and/or battery or the statutory offence of assault occasioning actual bodily harm under the Offences Against A Person Act 1861.

In the case of sexual harassment, extreme cases may also involve indecent assault. By way of example, in *R* v. *Wakefield & Lancashire* (CA, 6 November 2000), the Criminal Division of the Court of Appeal upheld two convictions of indecent assault, involving custodial sentences of 12 and 21 months, where two employees had subjected a female colleague to a series of regular physical assaults of a sexual nature. The victim was forced to leave her employment and suffered from severe depression as a result of these assaults. The Court of Appeal held that this was a case of public sexual bullying and involved a prolonged period of humiliating and degrading treatment.

Such extreme cases are, thankfully, rare but, even if a criminal prosecution is successful, the victim will not be able to recover substantial compensation via this route.

Public Order Act 1986

Under s.4A of the Public Order Act 1986, it is a criminal offence to intentionally harass someone and, potentially, this offence could apply to harassment in the workplace.

The offence requires proof of intent to cause harassment, alarm or distress by using threatening, abusive or insulting language or behaviour, or disorderly behaviour, or displaying any writing, sign or other visible representation which is threatening, abusive or insulting, so that another person feels harassment, alarm or distress.

The maximum penalty is a term of imprisonment not exceeding 6 months and/or a fine not exceeding level 5 on the standard scale. Racial or religious aggravation may increase the term of imprisonment to up to 2 years.

Again, as this is a criminal offence, it is not attractive route for victims to pursue if they are looking for financial recompense, as it will not help them to get much in the way of compensation, there being no civil remedy under the Act.

Protection from Harassment Act 1997

The Protection from Harassment Act 1997 was introduced primarily to deal with the problem of stalking, but it could also apply to bullying and harassment in the workplace. 'Harassment' is defined by the Act as including conduct which causes the victim alarm or distress.

Under s.2 of the Act, it is an offence for a person to pursue a course of conduct which amounts to harassment of another and which he knows or ought to know amounts to harassment of the other. The offence carries a maximum prison sentence of 6 months and/or a fine not exceeding level 5 on the standard scale.

Under s.4 of the Act, there is a higher-level offence where a person pursues a course of conduct which he knows or ought to know causes another person to fear, on at least two occasions, that violence will be used against him. This offence carries a maximum term of imprisonment of 5 years and/or a fine.

The interesting point about this Act is that, as well as making such actions criminal, it also provides a civil remedy for the victim. Damages may be awarded for any anxiety caused by the harassment and any financial loss resulting from the harassment. This could include damages not only for any psychiatric injury suffered, but also for any anxiety and stress caused to the victim falling short of a recognised psychiatric illness.

However, the Act has proved to be of little application in the employment field, primarily because of the difficulties in interpreting its definitions and due to the fact that a complainant has to prove a course of conduct, i.e. that the harassment occurred on repeated occasions. If a stalker is pursuing someone, the victim is likely to be able to identify the dates on which the stalking occurred and the acts complained of. In the workplace context, it may be that an employee feels he has been humiliated in front of his colleagues or that he has been disciplined or reprimanded without cause, but the course of conduct is usually going to be far less clearly definable.

The real difficulty with this Act is that of fixing responsibility for the harassment on the employer, who is more likely to be able to pay substantial compensation than the harasser. The employer will only be liable if it has aided and abetted the harasser. Arguably, an employer who has no policies in place to deal with harassment, ignores complaints or promotes and praises the harasser, might fall into this category, but it does seem a fairly high hurdle to cross.

From a practical point of view, although this Act can theoretically be used to deal with workplace bullying and harassment, there are usually better options for a victim of workplace harassment to pursue.

Negligence

An employee who has suffered a diagnosed psychiatric illness as a result of bullying and harassment at work could bring a claim against his employer for damages for personal injury. Claims in negligence for personal injury are discussed in more detail in **Chapters 2** and **3**.

Health and safety legislation

Employers have a duty to provide a safe working environment for their employees and permitting an environment in which bullying and harassment can thrive could be in breach of this obligation. An employer's liability for health and safety is examined in more detail in **Chapter 5**.

Discrimination

As indicated earlier in this chapter, if the victim of bullying and harassment is protected by one of the discrimination Acts, i.e. the harassment is on the grounds of sex, race or disability, then it may be possible for the employee to bring a discrimination claim. Such a claim could be brought both against the perpetrator of the behaviour and the employer and, as well as compensating the employee for loss of earnings, it could also give rise to compensation in respect of any stress, anxiety or distress caused, whether or not this amounted to a recognised psychiatric disorder, i.e. injury to feelings.

The SDA and the DDA do not mention specifically the term 'harassment', although the RRA now does, but the Employment Tribunals have interpreted these Acts as covering harassment and recognised that harassment can be a form of discrimination.

Under s.1(1)(a) of the SDA, a person discriminates against a woman if, on the grounds of her sex, he treats her less favourably than he treats or would treat a man. The SDA applies equally to discrimination against men. Section 5(1) of the DDA contains a similar provision in respect of disability discrimination.

The SDA has been amended to cover individuals undergoing gender reassignment, but it does not cover discrimination on the grounds of sexual orientation unless it can be shown that, for example, a male homosexual was harassed because of his homosexuality but a female homosexual would not have been subjected to like harassment (see *Smith* v. *Gardner Merchant Limited* [1998] IRLR 510, CA).

Under s.6(2)(b) of the SDA, it is unlawful for an employer to discriminate against an employee by dismissing him or subjecting him to any other detriment (see also s.4(2)(d) of the DDA). Detriment means a disadvantage of some kind and harassment can be a detriment if it is such that a reasonable employee would or might feel disadvantaged in the circumstances and conditions in which he has to work (see *De Souza* v. *Automobile Association* [1986] IRLR 103, EAT).

If harassment is proved, the harasser will be personally liable for his acts of discrimination. However, if his actions were carried out in the course of his employment, they will be treated as having been done by his employer as well as by him, whether or not those actions were done with the employer's knowledge or approval (s.41(1) of the SDA, s.32(1) of the RRA and s.58(1) of the DDA). This test is different from the test of vicarious liability in negligence and, in the majority of cases, the employer is unlikely to escape liability.

The purpose of the discrimination legislation is to deter discrimination in the workplace by widening the net of responsibility beyond making employees liable for their own actions, but also making employers additionally liable for harassment, unless they have used their best endeavours to prevent such harassment occurring. Even where the harassment in question could not in any sense be said to be a mode of doing what the harasser is employed to do, the employer can still be liable, otherwise the more heinous the act of discrimination, the less likely it would be that the employer would be liable (see *Jones* v. *Tower Boot Company Limited* [1997] IRLR 168, CA and *Bracebridge Engineering Limited* v. *Darby* [1990] IRLR 3, EAT).

An employer may even be liable for the acts of its employees which take place outside the workplace, if the event is connected with work or the workplace, for example harassment that takes place at an office party or during a drink after work (see *Chief Constable of the Lincolnshire Police* v. *Stubbs* [1999] IRLR 81, EAT).

An employer can also be liable for the acts of third parties if it has control over a particular event or set of circumstances and fails to take steps to prevent the harassment taking place or to reduce the extent of it (see *Burton & Rhule* v. *De Vere Hotels* [1996] IRLR 596, EAT and *Bennett* v. *Essex County Council and the Chair and Governors of Fryern's School & Hayes*, EAT, 5 October 1999).

The defence to such claims is to show that the employer took all steps that were reasonably practicable to prevent the harassment by the employee or third party. This involves identifying whether the employer took any steps to prevent the harassment and then considering whether there were any further steps which the employer could have taken which were reasonably practicable (see *Canniffe* v. *East Riding of Yorkshire Council* [2000] IRLR 555, EAT).

It is not critical to show that such steps would have prevented the harassment occurring; the fact that the employer failed to take reasonably practicable steps, even if they would have made no difference, can be enough to establish the employer's liability.

An employee alleging that he has been harassed contrary to the SDA, the RRA or the DDA may bring a discrimination claim in the Employment Tribunals. Such a claim should be brought within three months of the act complained of, or within such further period as the Employment Tribunal considers just and equitable in the circumstances. There is no qualifying period of service necessary in order to bring such a claim.

The Employment Tribunal can make one or more of the following awards:

1. A declaration as to the rights of the parties.
2. A recommendation that the employer takes certain action within a specified period for the purpose of avoiding or reducing the adverse effects of the discrimination, e.g. introducing an equal opportunities policy.
3. Compensation, including an award for loss of earnings and an award for injury to feelings. There is no statutory cap on the compensation that can be awarded.

In assessing an award for injury to feelings, the Employment Tribunal should look at the circumstances objectively with reference to what any ordinary person would feel and subjectively with reference to the individual. The compensation awarded should relate to the degree of detriment actually suffered by the individual (see *Snowball* v. *Gardner Merchant Limited* [1987] IRLR 397, EAT).

In recent years, awards for injury to feelings have become less predictable and some very large sums have been awarded (see *Whitehead* v. *Isle of Wight NHS Trust*, EAT, 25 August 1999 and *Virdi* v. *Commissioner of Police for the Metropolis*, EAT, 8 December 2000).

However, the Court of Appeal has recently set down guidelines to be used in assessing awards for injury to feelings in discrimination cases in *Vento* v. *Chief Constable of West Yorkshire Police* [2003] IRLR 102. Three bands of compensation have been identified. The top band of £15,000–25,000 should only be used for the most serious cases, such as those involving a lengthy campaign of harassment. Compensation above this level for injury to feelings should only be awarded in the most exceptional of circumstances. The mid band of £5,000–15,000 should be used in cases that do not merit the top band. The bottom band of £500–5,000 should be used in less serious cases, such as those involving an isolated or one-off incident. Awards of under £500 should be avoided, as this would not be a proper recognition of injury to feelings.

Awards for injury to feelings can include compensation for psychiatric illness brought about by the discriminatory treatment, whether or not this was reasonably foreseeable (see *Sheriff* v. *Klyne Tugs Lowestoft Limited* [1999] IRLR 481, CA). However, double recovery in a discrimination claim and a negligence claim is not permitted.

The Employment Tribunal can also award aggravated damages if, for example, an employer adds to an employee's stress by strongly defending a claim when it knows it has no reasonable prospect of successfully defending it.

Constructive dismissal

Discrimination law protects employees from bullying and harassment at work to the extent that they fall within a protected category and establish that the harassment was on the grounds of their race, sex or disability. However, the discrimination legislation will not assist those who fall outside these protected categories and there are likely to be fewer options available for such individuals if they wish to bring legal proceedings.

An employer owes a number of duties to its employees, including the duty to provide a safe place of work, the duty to protect employees' health and the duty not to behave in a manner calculated or likely to destroy the relationship of trust and confidence without reasonable or proper cause. These duties are terms implied into every contract of employment and a breach of one or more of these duties may be a fundamental breach of the contract of employment, entitling the employee to resign and claim constructive dismissal.

An employee suffering bullying and harassment may use constructive dismissal as the basis for bringing a claim if his employer has failed in its duty by exposing him to such behaviour, or it has failed to deal with a complaint seriously.

Often there is little alternative for employees but to bring a claim for constructive dismissal. However, the main drawback is that it involves taking the drastic step of resigning and walking out of a job, leaving the employee with no earnings and uncertain prospects of being awarded adequate compensation even if his claim is successful.

A claim for constructive dismissal would usually involve a claim for breach of contract and a claim for unfair dismissal. Compensation for breach of contract is normally limited to the net salary and benefits the employee would have received during his contractual notice period.

In order to bring a claim for unfair dismissal, the employee would need to have a year's qualifying service. Compensation for unfair dismissal could include damages for future loss, but no compensation would be awarded for any psychiatric injury suffered.

Constructive dismissal is examined in more detail in **Chapter 9**.

7.6   PRACTICAL STEPS TO PREVENT BULLYING AND HARASSMENT

Creating a positive working environment can not only avoid the possibility of any successful legal claims being brought against an employer, but can have significant business advantages. The basic steps that an employer can take to protect itself from bullying and harassment can be summed up in two words: good management.

Practical steps would be to:

- carry out a risk assessment;
- implement an equal opportunities policy;
- implement a bullying and harassment policy;
- use and monitor these policies;
- provide awareness training for managers and staff;
- train line managers on how to handle complaints;
- consider having a nominated officer to deal with complaints;
- demonstrate that complaints are handled promptly and sensitively;
- provide counselling for complainants.

It is important that employees know that bullying and harassment will not be tolerated in the workplace. If this is made clear in a bullying and harassment policy, this will deter employees from acting in an unacceptable manner and will encourage victims to come forward, so that these issues can be dealt with and resolved.

It is usually not appropriate to deal with bullying and harassment under a grievance procedure, as these types of issues require very sensitive handling. Therefore, the adoption of a bullying and harassment policy is advisable. Such a policy should encourage the resolution of these types of issues informally, if possible, but provide a formal procedure for those issues that cannot be resolved informally or are too serious to be dealt with under an informal procedure.

A bullying and harassment policy should make it clear that bullying and harassment are unacceptable forms of conduct and will not be condoned. It should define bullying and harassment and give examples of the kind of behaviour that will be regarded as unacceptable. A policy should place a positive duty on employees to

81

comply with it and to ensure that their colleagues are treated with dignity. The responsibilities of those who witness bullying and harassment should also be made clear.

It is important that a bullying and harassment policy makes it clear to whom employees should complain and how, if they are victims of such behaviour, and that the employer is seen to deal with such matters seriously, expeditiously and confidentially. It should be expressly made clear that any breach of the policy could result in disciplinary action being taken against the perpetrator.

However, having a bullying and harassment policy is not enough in itself. The policy needs to be drawn to the attention of employees and they should receive appropriate training on it. Managers should be trained to look for signs of bullying and harassment and to investigate where appropriate.

It is also necessary to support the policy with a continuous programme of communication and awareness across the organisation and to continually review the operation of the policy in practice.

7.7 THE FUTURE

Forthcoming UK legislation

On 2 December 2003, legislation is to be introduced outlawing discrimination on the grounds of sexual orientation and religion and belief and draft Regulations have now been published. This will be followed, in 2006, by legislation to deal with the issue of age discrimination, upon which the Government is currently consulting.

This new legislation will expand the number of protected categories under UK discrimination law. It will provide statutory definitions of harassment on these grounds and will mean that harassment on the grounds of sexual orientation, religion and belief and age will give rise to discrimination claims in the same way as discrimination on the grounds of sex, race and disability currently gives rise to liability.

European legislation

In September 2002, the EU Equal Treatment Directive (76/207/EEC) was amended by Directive 2002/73/EC, which, when it is implemented, will, for the first time, introduce a formal legal definition of sexual harassment:

Where any form of unwanted verbal, non-verbal or physical conduct of a sexual nature occurs, with the purpose or effect of violating the dignity of a person, in particular when creating an intimidating, hostile, degrading, humiliating or offensive environment.

The Directive is due to be implemented by 5 October 2005, from which date sexual harassment will be deemed to be discrimination on the grounds of sex and will be prohibited under EU law. Employers will be obliged by this legislation to take a proactive approach to preventing sexual harassment in the workplace.

Other developments

In 1997, the Manufacturing Science and Finance Union (now Amicus) produced a Dignity at Work Bill. The Bill, if passed, would give every employee the right to dignity at work and make employers liable for any breach of this right, including offensive, abusive, malicious, insulting and intimidating behaviour. It would enable employees to bring complaints in the Employment Tribunals for breach of this right without them having to resign and claim constructive dismissal.

The Bill ran out of parliamentary time before it was passed, but started its progress again in 2001, backed by Amicus. Although it has now progressed through the House of Lords and had its first reading in the House of Commons, there are no current proposals to devote more parliamentary time to it and it is unlikely to become law in the foreseeable future.

7.8 CONCLUSION

Although bullying and harassment in the workplace are two of the main causes of stress and stress-related illnesses, establishing liability for them and obtaining compensation is by no means straightforward.

At present, the main remedies for employees who are subjected to such behaviour are to be found through the Employment Tribunals, either by way of harassment claims under the discrimination legislation or through constructive dismissal claims.

Employers can do a lot to protect themselves against such claims by having good policies and procedures in place, ensuring that people are aware of them and training managers to spot difficulties in this area and to handle complaints sensitively. The benefits of a proactive approach to bullying and harassment extend beyond the avoidance of successful legal claims and can help to provide a much more positive working environment, with the commercial advantages this can bring.

CHAPTER 8

Dismissal

8.1 INTRODUCTION

Some individuals suffering from stress-related illness can continue to work and their capability to carry out their jobs will be unaffected. However, in many cases, a stress-related illness can cause an employee to have long periods of sick leave, or it may result in frequent intermittent absences. Alternatively, such an illness may not affect the employee's ability to attend work, but may affect his capability to do the job whilst he is there.

The employer of an employee who is suffering from a stress-related illness is likely to face a number of practical difficulties. Although a sympathetic and compassionate approach should be adopted throughout the period of illness, at some stage the employer may decide that a more permanent solution has to be found and that termination of the contract of employment should be considered. So, how and when can the contract of employment be brought to an end and what steps should the employer take to avoid liability?

8.2 FRUSTRATION

In extreme circumstances, an illness may frustrate a contract of employment, i.e. make it incapable of being performed through no fault of either party (see *Davis Contractors Limited* v. *Fareham Urban District Council* [1956] AC 696, HL). In such circumstances, the contract will terminate by operation of law and there will be no dismissal, so there can be no liability for breach of contract or unfair dismissal arising out of termination.

The test is whether the illness is of such a nature, or appears likely to continue for such a period, that further performance of the employee's obligations would be either impossible or radically different from that agreed in the contract of employment (see *Marshall* v. *Harland & Wolff Limited* [1972] IRLR 90, NIRC). For example, if there is a medical opinion to the effect that the employee will never be able to work again and is permanently unable to perform the contract of employment, then the contract is likely to be frustrated (see *Notcutt* v. *Universal Equipment Co (London) Limited* [1986] IRLR 218, CA).

However, in practice, the courts and Employment Tribunals are reluctant to treat a contract of employment as frustrated by an employee's illness. In *Williams* v. *Watsons Luxury Coaches Limited* [1990] IRLR 164, the EAT warned that the courts should guard against too easy an application of the doctrine of frustration, as it can harm good industrial relations and provide an easy escape from the obligations of a conscientious employer.

The use of the doctrine of frustration in long-term sickness situations also appears to be inconsistent with the approach taken by the courts in relation to permanent health insurance claims (for further details, see **Chapter 9**), where it has been held that an employer is not entitled to dismiss an employee if this would terminate the employee's entitlement to benefits under a permanent health insurance scheme, never mind treat the contract as frustrated (see *Aspden* v. *Webbs Poultry & Meat Group (Holdings) Limited* [1996] IRLR 521, HC).

Only in the most exceptional of circumstances will a contract become frustrated due to a stress-related illness and it could be dangerous for an employer to rely on the doctrine of frustration as terminating the contract in these types of cases. More usually, the contract will need to be terminated by way of dismissal and the potential liability arising out of ill-health dismissals is analysed in this chapter.

8.3 BREACH OF CONTRACT

Every employee, regardless of his length of service, has the right not to be dismissed in breach of his contract of employment. This generally means that the employee has the right to be dismissed on due notice, provided that he is not in repudiatory breach of his contract of employment, entitling the employer to dismiss him summarily.

Notice periods

When dealing with a dismissal on the grounds of a stress-related illness, it is important that the employer establishes what period of notice the employee is entitled to. There may be a contractual notice period but, if the contract is silent on this point, or if the contractual notice period is shorter than that required by statute, the statutory minimum notice periods under s.86 of the Employment Rights Act 1996 ('the ERA') will apply.

The statutory minimum notice periods to be given by an employer to an employee are one week's notice for continuous service of between 1 month and 2 years and, thereafter, 1 week's notice for each year of continuous service, up to a maximum of 12 weeks' notice after 12 years. It is not possible to contract out of these minimum periods, although the parties can, of course, agree more generous notice periods should they so wish.

A contract of employment may entitle the employer to terminate the contract immediately and pay the employee in lieu of notice but, in the absence of such a clause, if the contract is terminated without due notice, the employer will be acting in breach of contract.

Calculation of damages

The aim of damages for breach of contract is to put the employee in the position he would have been in had the contract been performed. This means that the calculation is usually based on the net salary and benefits the employee would have received if he had been given due notice, subject to the employee's duty to mitigate his loss. However, mitigation is less likely to be an issue in cases of continuing ill health than in relation to dismissals for other reasons.

Where an employee is absent from work due to a stress-related illness, he may have exhausted his right to contractual or statutory sick pay. In these circumstances, the question will be what, if any, compensation will the employee be entitled to if he is dismissed in breach of contract or what should the employee be paid during his notice period if the employer dismisses him on notice?

If the employee is only entitled to the statutory minimum period of notice, then, under s.88 of the ERA, the employee is entitled to be paid full pay during his notice period, even if he is incapable of working during this period due to illness and even if he has no entitlement to or has exhausted his entitlement to contractual sick pay. Any contractual or statutory sick pay will go towards meeting the employer's liability in these circumstances. Any damages for breach of contract in this situation would, therefore, be based on full pay and benefits during the notice period, subject to the duty to mitigate.

However, if the employee's contractual notice period is one week or more longer than his statutory notice entitlement, then, under s.87(4) of the ERA, no pay has to be paid to the employee if he is off sick during his notice period, other than any contractual or statutory sick pay which is due. Therefore, if an employee with such a longer period of contractual notice entitlement is dismissed without notice, having exhausted his right to sick pay, he may not be able to recover any damages for breach of contract.

Remedies

A claim for breach of contract, whether in respect of a contractual or statutory notice period, can be brought in an Employment Tribunal within three months of the dismissal, if the compensation sought is under £25,000. Alternatively, a breach of contract claim can be brought in the High Court or County Court within six years of the dismissal, where there is no financial cap on the compensation recoverable.

The choice of venue in which the claim is brought will usually depend on the value of the claim, the speed with which the employee wants it to be dealt with, whether an unfair dismissal claim is also being brought and the likelihood of recovering costs from the employer.

Other contractual claims

If an employer's sickness policy or procedure is incorporated into the contract of employment, then an employee may also have a breach of contract claim against his employer if it fails to comply with the terms of the contract. So, if the employee is dismissed without the employer first going through the correct contractual procedure, he may be able to recover compensation not only in respect of the failure by the employer to give due notice, but also for the period of time it would have taken for the employer to go through the contractual procedure.

Similarly, the termination of an employee's contract of employment on the grounds of ill health whilst the employee is still entitled to receive contractual sick pay would have the effect of subverting the employee's rights to sick pay under the contract and could give rise to a claim based, not only on lack of notice, but also in respect of the unexpired period of sick pay entitlement (see *Hill* v. *General Accident Fire & Life Assurance Corporation plc* [1998] IRLR 641, Court of Session).

The potentially substantial liability for breach of contract arising out of the dismissal of an employee on the grounds of ill health when the employee has an entitlement to benefits under a permanent health insurance scheme is discussed in detail in **Chapter 9**.

8.4 UNFAIR DISMISSAL

'Incapability'

Any dismissal of an employee on the grounds of a stress-related illness may also give rise to a claim for unfair dismissal. Section 94 of the ERA sets out the statutory right not to be unfairly dismissed, which is separate and distinct from any contractual rights. Normally, employees will only be entitled to bring a claim for unfair dismissal if they have 12 months' continuous service at the date of the termination of their employment (s.108 of the ERA).

Section 98 of the ERA sets out the five potentially fair reasons for dismissal. With stress-related illnesses, the reason will usually be capability, which includes the employee's health and physical and mental qualities.

Once the employer has established a potentially fair reason for dismissal under s.98(4) of the ERA, whether or not the dismissal was, in fact, fair is a question to be determined by the Employment Tribunal taking into account all the circumstances, including the size and administrative resources of the undertaking and whether the employer acted reasonably in treating the reason as sufficient reason for dismissing the employee. This should be determined in accordance with equity and the substantial merits of the case. Every case will depend on its own facts.

Dismissal must fall within the reasonable band of responses open to the employer and the importance of following a fair procedure before taking the step of dismissing an employee on the grounds of ill health cannot be overemphasised.

The approach adopted by the employer when considering whether dismissal is appropriate in the particular circumstances may be different, depending on whether the employee continues to work but is obviously not capable of doing the job, is absent intermittently due to his health, or is on long-term sick leave.

Inability to perform the role

When dealing with an employee who appears to be unable to carry out the functions of his job because of his stress-related illness, although he does continue to attend work, the employer should review the situation with the employee and warn or caution the employee that if his performance does not improve then it will have to consider whether his employment can continue. The employer should also attempt to obtain medical evidence to support his decision and alternatives to dismissal should be considered.

Where the employee's ill health is caused by his work or his job is a major contributing factor, the employer may be under a duty to dismiss the employee rather than letting him continue to run the risk of physical or psychological injury (see *Coxall* v. *Goodyear GB Limited* [2002] IRLR 742, CA). Similarly, if an employee's illness makes him a danger to others, this may mean that his dismissal is justified (see *Harper* v. *National Coal Board* [1980] IRLR 260, EAT). However, such cases will be rare and, even in such circumstances, a proper consideration of all the circumstances is necessary and a fair procedure should be followed.

Persistent short-term absences

When dealing with an employee who is persistently absent from work for short periods of time due to a stress-related illness, the employer should review his attendance record and the reasons given for the absences. The employee should then be given an opportunity to state his case and, if appropriate, he should be warned that if his attendance does not improve then the employer will have to consider whether his employment can continue (see *International Sport Co* v. *Thomson* [1980] IRLR 340, EAT).

These warnings should not be akin to warnings under a disciplinary procedure, but should take the form of cautions and the employer's approach should be based on sympathy, understanding and compassion (see *Lynock* v. *Cereal Packaging Limited* [1988] IRLR 510, EAT).

Often with persistent short-term absences, medical evidence will not be of much assistance to an employer in reaching a decision. However, it may help to identify any underlying stress-related condition, so the employer should consider whether or not to obtain a medical report in the particular circumstances of the case.

Long-term sickness

With an employee on long-term sick leave due to a stress-related illness, the approach will essentially be for the employer to obtain as much information about the situation as possible, including medical evidence, so that it can then make a reasoned and fair decision after assessing all the facts and consulting with the employee.

Medical evidence

Before making any decision about the continued employment of an employee suffering from a stress-related illness, the employer should usually attempt to obtain medical evidence about the employee's condition, to ensure that it has all the necessary information available to it before reaching a decision. Although the decision to dismiss is ultimately a management one, and not a medical one, medical evidence will normally form a key factor in making such a decision.

If sought early on in an illness, a medical opinion can be of great assistance to an employer in making arrangements to cover the employee's absence. It may also help to establish how long the employee's illness is likely to last and to identify any steps that could be taken to facilitate the employee's early return to work, so that the possibility of dismissal does not have to be considered.

Normally, the first port of call for obtaining medical evidence will be the employee's general practitioner or consultant. The employer should write to the employee, requesting his consent to its contacting his doctor and explaining that the purpose of such contact is to obtain a report regarding the employee's state of health and when, if at all, he is likely to be able to return to work.

An employer seeking a report from a medical practitioner who is or has been responsible for the clinical care of the employee, i.e. the employee's own doctor, will have to comply with the Access to Medical Reports Act 1988. The Act protects the employee's right to withhold medical information from his employer and it helps to ensure that any information provided by the employee's doctor is correct. The procedure involves obtaining the employee's consent, allowing the employee the opportunity to see the report before it is sent to the employer and allowing the employee the right to request alterations and amendments to the report before it is supplied to the employer.

Rights under the Access to Medical Reports Act 1988 are that:

- the employee must be informed of his rights under the Act;
- the employee can consent or withhold consent;
- consent must be in writing;
- the employee can ask to see a copy of the report before it is sent to the employer;
- the employer must notify the doctor if the employee wants to see the report;
- the doctor may refuse to show the employee any part of the report which:

  - is likely to cause serious harm to the employee's health,
  - indicates the doctor's intentions towards the employee, or
  - contains information about another person who has supplied information about the employee;

- the employee may ask the doctor to amend any part of the report or have a statement attached to it setting out the employee's view as to the discrepancies;
- having seen the report, the employee can refuse to consent to its disclosure to the employer;
- the doctor may charge a fee;
- the employee may request sight of the report up to six months after its supply.

The Access to Health Records Act 1990 goes one step further and allows an employee to consent to his employer having direct access to most of his health records. The Act does not necessarily allow the employee himself to have access to these records.

As an alternative to approaching the employee's own doctor, the employer may want the employee to be examined by its own doctor or one instructed by it for this purpose. The advantages of a report from the employer's own doctor or an occupational health specialist are that they are more likely to have an understanding of the type of work which the employee is employed to do and to be able to relate the employee's illness to the particular requirements of his job. It is also an opportunity to get a second opinion on the employee's condition.

When instructing a doctor to produce a medical report, whether this is the employee's doctor or one instructed by the employer, it is important to include details of the nature of the employee's job and his duties. Specific questions should be asked about the nature of the employee's illness, its effects on the employee's ability to carry out his normal activities, the prognosis and whether there are any steps the employer can take to facilitate the employee's return to work. With an employee on long-term sick leave, the employer will want to know whether or not the employee is likely to make a complete recovery and, if so, when, to enable it to take a decision about whether it is practical to wait for the employee to return to work, or whether a decision about the employee's continued employment should be made at this stage.

As a general rule, if the employee refuses to consent to the employer's obtaining a report from his own doctor or refuses to consent to a medical examination by the employer's doctor, the employer will have to proceed on the basis of the evidence available to it. The employer cannot insist on the employee's consent to its obtaining a medical report or to his undergoing a medical examination. If the employee refuses consent, the employer should write to him, stating that, in the absence of medical evidence, it will have to act on the facts available to it, even if those facts are insufficient to ascertain the full medical position. However, employers may want to consider inserting a clause into their contracts of employment specifically requiring employees to undergo a medical examination should the employer request it. Any failure to do so would then be a breach of contract on the part of the employee and could be dealt with as a disciplinary issue.

If the employer is faced with conflicting medical reports, it may be acting reasonably if it relies on one report rather than the other, provided that it has good reasons for doing so, particularly where the medical opinion relied upon is less favourable to the employee. However, if in doubt, the employer would be best advised to get a third opinion.

There is no general obligation on an employer to obtain a medical report from a specialist but, in some circumstances, it should be considered, for example if a report from the employee's general practitioner is inconclusive or if the employer is aware that the employee is undergoing specialist treatment.

The medical position is obviously extremely important, but it is not the sole consideration and it should be considered in conjunction with consultation with the employee.

Duty to consult

Before reaching any decision about the employee's continued employment, the employer should consult with the employee. This will help to establish the true medical position and will also help the employer weigh up the situation, balancing its need to get the work done against the employee's need to have time to recover without the threat of losing his job. Only in exceptional circumstances will it be fair to dismiss an employee on the grounds of ill health without first discussing the matter with him, as such consultation may bring to light facts and circumstances of which the employer was previously unaware and throw new light on the problem (see *East Lindsey District Council* v. *Daubrey* [1977] IRLR 181, EAT).

Such a review could help to dispel any preconceptions the employer may have about the employee's illness and may, for example, identify any physical as well as mental problems arising out of the employee's illness and any workplace stressors which may be causing or exacerbating the employee's illness. A practical approach should be adopted and, in some cases, fairly simple and inexpensive steps could be taken to alleviate the stress the employee is suffering.

Consultation should not take the form of a warning, which carries with it connotations that the employee is being required to change or improve his conduct which, in the case of a genuinely ill employee, it is not within his power to do. Consultation should start as early as possible during the illness and should continue throughout it, particularly once the employer has obtained medical evidence. The onus is on the employer to consult and seek out information, and not on the employee to volunteer such information (see *Mitchell* v. *Arkwood Plastics (Engineering) Limited* [1993] ICR 471, EAT).

In stress-related cases, a careful balance has to be struck between concerned consultation and pestering the employee, thus adding to his stress. However, with careful handling, this should be possible. It may be inappropriate to expect the employee to attend a formal meeting in these circumstances and often a meeting at the employee's home or at a neutral venue will be preferable to one in the workplace.

The employer should discuss with the employee the nature of the illness, the impact it has on the employee, the prognosis and when the employee considers he will be able to return to work. The parties should also discuss any steps that could be taken to facilitate the employee's return to work, such as a phased return or a return to a less stressful position, whether on a temporary or permanent basis. The employer should make the employee aware of the problems it is experiencing during his absence. If dismissal is being considered, this should be explained to the employee and the reasons for it and alternatives should also be discussed.

Considering alternatives

Alternative employment should be considered if work exists which the employee may be able to do, but there is no duty to create a new job for the employee where none exists. However, the obligation may be more onerous if the employee is disabled and the employer has to consider what reasonable adjustments could be made (see **Chapter 6**). There may be other alternatives to dismissal, such as early ill-health retirement, which should also be considered.

Decision to dismiss

Once medical evidence has been obtained and consultation has taken place with the employee, the employer then has to reach a decision based on all the facts. It may be that there is nothing more that the employer can do and that it has reached the point of no return, in which case the dismissal is likely to be fair. However, if, on the other hand, it is likely that the employee will be able to return to work in the near future and the employer could accommodate the employee's absence until then, the dismissal is likely to be unfair.

Most cases will fall somewhere in the middle and whether the dismissal is justified will involve a careful assessment of the facts, weighing up a variety of factors before the employer comes to a reasonable decision. It is important to remember that it is not for an Employment Tribunal to substitute its own view of what it would have done in the situation; the employer only has to act reasonably in the circumstances.

Every case will depend on its own facts, but the basic question will be whether, in all the circumstances, the employer can wait any longer before dismissing the employee and, if so, how long it should be expected to wait (see *Spencer* v. *Paragon Wallpapers Limited* [1976] IRLR 373, EAT). The size of the employer is usually going to be a very persuasive factor in determining whether a dismissal is fair. A small employer is far less likely to be able to absorb the impact of the absence of one of its key employees for a significant period of time than a larger employer with more resources available to deal with such an absence.

If the illness has been caused by or contributed to by the employee's workplace, as may be the case with many stress-related illnesses, the employer may be expected to adopt a more sympathetic approach than it might otherwise do before deciding to dismiss the employee. When considering the fairness of a dismissal the Employment Tribunal can take into account the fact that the employer caused or contributed to the illness (see *Edwards* v. *Governors of Hanson School* and *Frewin* v. *Consignia plc*, EAT, 18 July 2003).

Whether the employee has exhausted his right to contractual sick pay is also a factor to be taken into consideration by the employer. A dismissal whilst the employee is still in receipt of contractual sick pay will not necessarily be unfair (see *Coulson* v. *Felixstowe Dock & Railway Co* [1974] IRLR 11, IT), but it will not necessarily be fair to dismiss the employee once his entitlement to contractual sick pay has been exhausted (see *Hardwick* v. *Leeds Area Health Authority* [1975] IRLR 319, IT). However, if an employee's contract provides for sick pay for a specified period then, as the contract anticipates the possibility of absence for this period, it may be unfair to take steps to dismiss the employee before the entitlement to sick pay has expired.

The timing of the dismissal is a matter for the employer and there is no magic time after which a dismissal will be fair, it will depend on all the circumstances. However, consistency of treatment between employees is important; so as far as possible a standard approach should be adopted to ill-health dismissals.

If and when the time eventually comes when all procedures have been exhausted, all avenues explored and the employment cannot be kept open any longer, the employee should not be left in ignorance and should be informed as soon as possible of the employer's decision and the reasons for it.

Some factors to consider when determining whether to dismiss are the:

- nature and effect of the illness;
- cause of the illness;
- likely duration of the illness;
- likelihood of recurrence;
- length of the absence and any periods of good health in between;
- need of the employer to have the work done by the employee;
- feasibility of finding a temporary replacement;
- impact of the absence on other employees;

- employee's length of service;
- extent to which the employer's difficulties have been explained to the employee.

Appeal

If a decision is ultimately taken to dismiss the employee, it is important to remember that the employee should be offered the opportunity of appealing against this decision. The appeal should, ideally, be to a higher level of management than that which took the decision to dismiss and an appeal hearing should take place.

How to bring/defend a claim

A claim for unfair dismissal can only be brought in the Employment Tribunals. Under s.111 of the ERA, a claim should be brought within three months of the effective date of termination, or, if it is not reasonably practicable to bring a claim within this time limit, within such further period as the Employment Tribunal considers reasonable.

There are currently standard forms of application and response in tribunal proceedings, but it is not compulsory to use these. Proceedings can be started and defended using any written format. An application must give details of the applicant and the respondent and specify the grounds on which relief is sought. The response must give the respondent's details, state whether it intends to defend the claim and give the grounds for doing so.

However, under the Employment Act 2002, there is a power to make regulations prescribing the form in which proceedings are brought and defended and it is expected that such regulations will soon be introduced, with the aim of ensuring that more information is available to the parties and the Employment Tribunal at the commencement of proceedings, to assist in case management and promote settlement.

Remedies

An Employment Tribunal can order that the employee should be reinstated to the role he held prior to the dismissal or that he should be re-engaged on such terms and conditions as the Employment Tribunal determines. However, such orders are extremely rare in practice.

Compensation for unfair dismissal consists of two elements:

1. A basic award based on the employee's age, length of service and weekly wages.
2. A compensatory award calculated based on the employee's actual loss. This is subject to a statutory cap, currently £53,500.

Compensation for unfair dismissal is limited to financial loss and non-pecuniary losses are not recoverable (see *Dunnachie* v. *Kingston upon Hull City Council*, EAT, 15 May 2003).

The employee is under a duty to mitigate his loss by attempting to find alternative employment. However, in the case of an employee suffering from stress or a stress-related illness, it is far less likely that he will be able to mitigate his loss than in the case of a dismissal for another reason.

Compensation can be reduced to take into account the conduct of the employee if it is just and equitable to do so. It is unusual for there to be contributory fault in an ill-health dismissal. However, if the employer took a decision to dismiss following the employee's failure to consent to a medical examination or report, even if the dismissal is ultimately found to have been unfair, this may reduce the amount of compensation recoverable.

8.5 DISABILITY DISCRIMINATION

Liability for disability discrimination is discussed in detail in **Chapter 6**. However, before dismissing an employee on the grounds of ill health, it is important to consider whether or not the employee is disabled and if he may be suffering from a disability, to take steps to minimise any potential liability.

Medical evidence and consultation with the employee are usually essential, both in establishing whether the employee is disabled and ascertaining whether there are any reasonable adjustments the employer can make to facilitate the employee's return to work. However, even if the employee is disabled, if no reasonable adjustments can be made, dismissal on capability grounds may be justified in appropriate circumstances.

8.6 CONCLUSION

An employer should have sickness policies and procedures in place to enable it to deal with ill-health issues fairly and consistently. As a general rule, no decision should be taken about an employee's continued employment until the medical position has been ascertained and consultation has taken place with the employee. In a situation where an employee is suffering from a stress-related illness, he should be dealt with sympathetically and with understanding and compassion and should only be dismissed once all the other options have been considered. If this is done, liability can be avoided.

CHAPTER 9

Other employment issues

9.1 INTRODUCTION

Elsewhere in this publication, an employer's potential liability in respect of disability discrimination, negligence, health and safety and bullying and harassment have been examined, as has the possibility of claims arising out of the dismissal of an employee on the grounds that he is suffering from a stress-related illness. However, stress can also give rise to a variety of other employment issues and the intention of this chapter is to examine some of these in more detail.

9.2 DISCIPLINARY/PERFORMANCE ISSUES

Disciplinary meetings

A common scenario in which the issue of workplace stress can arise is when an employer calls an employee to a disciplinary hearing or a meeting to discuss concerns about the employee's performance. If the employee then goes on sick leave, claiming to be suffering from stress, anxiety or some other stress-related ailment, the employer can find itself in a difficult position, wondering how best to proceed.

In this situation, the employer really has two options: proceed as it intended to before the employee's illness, perhaps with some adjustments to the procedure adopted; or wait until the employee returns to work before addressing the concerns. Both of these approaches have their down sides.

An employer, faced with a sick note for a stress-related illness, in these circumstances, may feel that it wants to establish whether the illness is genuine or whether the employee is using the excuse of an illness as a means of avoiding the meeting to address the employer's concerns. In order to do this, the employer should either seek the employee's consent to its obtaining a medical report from his doctor, or it should ask the employee to consent to a medical examination by the employer's doctor or one instructed by it for this purpose. However, care should be taken not to adopt too heavy-handed an approach because, if the illness is genuine, the fact that the employer seeks to establish that it is not may well add to the employee's stress and exacerbate or prolong his illness.

It should also be borne in mind that although the employee may not be fit to attend work, he might still be fit to attend the disciplinary/performance meeting. Again, care should be taken if the employer wishes to adopt this approach and it may well be advisable to obtain medical advice before proceeding with the meeting.

If the employee's illness appears likely to last for some time, the employer may want to consider going ahead with the disciplinary/ performance meeting anyway. If it does so, it should invite the employee to attend the meeting and also consider what adjustments could be made to the procedure to accommodate the employee's illness. It may be desirable to hold the meeting at a neutral venue rather than the workplace, to allow the employee to make written representations rather than attend the meeting in person, or to allow the employee to send along a representative to the meeting to present his case rather than attending himself. However, if the employee is dismissed following a meeting at which he has not attended himself, there will be a risk that the dismissal will be found to be unfair.

Returning to work

If an employer decides to put any concerns about conduct or performance to one side until the employee is well enough to return to work, it can be storing up problems for the future.

With the threat of a disciplinary/performance meeting hanging over him, the employee may well take longer to recover than he might otherwise do and, in some cases, the employee may be unable to return to work if it means that he will have to face the stress of such a meeting. The illness may then continue indefinitely and dismissal of the employee on the grounds of ill health may have to be considered at a later stage (see **Chapter 8**).

As time passes memories may fade and it may be more difficult to deal with the issues of concern when the employee returns to work due to lack of evidence or because matters have gone stale. This can be addressed to some extent by conducting an investigation and taking statements from witnesses whilst the employee is on sick leave, but having unresolved issues around may also have an effect on other members of staff and make working relationships untenable.

Whether it is best to go ahead with the hearing or wait for the employee's return will depend on the particular circumstances and what level of risk the employer is prepared to assume.

9.3 GRIEVANCES

The importance of an employer having a grievance procedure cannot be overemphasised when dealing with issues of workplace stress. If employees feel that they have a procedure whereby their complaints will be dealt with effectively, whether they be in relation to workplace conflicts or working conditions, this can prevent issues escalating to the stage where an employee's health suffers and it can help reduce the problems caused by stress at work.

However, having a grievance procedure is not enough; the employer must ensure that all employees are aware of the procedure, that managers are trained in how to operate it, that all grievances are properly and promptly investigated and that they are dealt with in a fair and appropriate manner. Employees should feel confident that if they have a grievance, they know who to talk to about it and that it will be dealt with appropriately.

Pursuant to the Employment Act 2002, a statutory grievance procedure will be implied into every contract of employment from October 2004. However, this statutory procedure is very basic and employers would be best advised to adopt a more detailed procedure, tailored to the requirements of their particular organisation.

9.4 CONSTRUCTIVE DISMISSAL

In **Chapter 8**, the possibility of an employer dismissing an employee on the grounds of a stress-related illness was considered and the possibility of an employee resigning and claiming constructive dismissal was touched upon when liability for bullying and harassment was examined in **Chapter 7**. However, there are a variety of circumstances in which an employee suffering from stress or a stress-related illness may feel that he has no choice but to resign from his job and claim that he has been constructively dismissed.

Definition

Under s.95(1)(c) of the Employment Rights Act 1996, an employee is constructively dismissed where he terminates the contract under which he is employed, with or without notice, in circumstances in which he is entitled to terminate it without notice by reason of the employer's conduct.

In order for the employee to treat himself as constructively dismissed and discharged from his contractual obligations, the employer's conduct has to be a significant breach of contract which goes to the root of the contract of employment, or which indicates that the employer no longer intends to be bound by one or more of the essential terms of the contract (see *Western Excavation (ECC) Ltd* v. *Sharp* [1978] IRLR 27, CA).

In order to succeed in a claim for constructive dismissal, four key elements have to be established:

- there must be a breach of contract by the employer;
- the breach must be sufficiently serious to justify the employee's resignation;
- the employee must resign in response to the breach; and
- the employee must not delay too long before resigning or he may be deemed to have affirmed the contract.

Breach of contract by the employer

Whether or not there has been a repudiatory breach of contract on the part of the employer will depend on all the circumstances. What may amount to a fundamental breach in some circumstances may not in others, so it is necessary to look at the facts of each particular situation.

There may be a breach of an express term, such as requiring an employee to work in excess of his contractual hours or unilaterally varying his contractual duties. However, breach of an implied term of a contract of employment, such as failing to provide a safe place of work, failing to protect an employee from bullying and harassment, or failing to give an employee reasonable support in performing his duties, could also give rise to a claim for constructive dismissal. However, the implied term, which is probably most commonly relied on in constructive dismissal claims, is the implied duty of mutual trust and confidence.

In *Courtaulds Northern Textiles Limited* v. *Andrew* [1979] IRLR 84, the EAT held that a term is implied into every contract of employment that the employer will not, without reasonable or proper cause, conduct itself in a manner calculated or likely to destroy or seriously damage the relationship of trust and confidence between the employer and the employee.

In establishing whether there has been a breach of the implied duty of trust and confidence, it is first necessary to establish whether there have been any acts by or on behalf of the employer which were likely, on their face, to seriously damage or destroy the relationship of trust and confidence and then it is necessary to establish whether there was any reasonable or proper cause for those acts (see *Hilton* v. *Shiner Limited – Builders Merchants* [2001] IRLR 727, EAT).

If the employer's conduct does amount to a breach of the implied term of trust and confidence, then that will inevitably mean that there has been a fundamental or repudiatory breach necessarily going to the root of the contract of employment (see *Morrow* v. *Safeway Stores plc* [2002] IRLR 9, EAT).

It is not necessary to show that the employer intended to breach the implied term of trust and confidence, but the employer's conduct must be looked at as a whole in determining whether its effect was such that, judged reasonably and sensibly, the employee could not have been expected to put up with it (see *Woods* v. *W M Car Services (Peterborough) Limited* [1981] IRLR 347, EAT).

Resignation in response to the breach

The reason or principal reason for the employee's resignation must be the employer's repudiatory breach of contract and, ideally, this should be communicated to the employer at the stage when the employee resigns or soon thereafter.

The fact that the employee does not make it clear, either by words or conduct, that he is resigning as a result of the employer's conduct is not fatal to a claim for constructive dismissal, because often employees do not want to confront their employer in these circumstances. However, the fact that the reason is not communicated by the employee to the employer at the time of the resignation may make it more difficult for the employee to prove that he was constructively dismissed (see *Weathershield Limited* v. *Sargent* [1999] IRLR 94, CA).

If the employer is in repudiatory breach of contract, the employee is entitled to leave without giving any notice at all. Alternatively, he can give notice and say that he is leaving at the end of the notice period. However, the conduct must be sufficiently serious to entitle him to leave at once.

Often in constructive dismissal cases, the employer's conduct will involve a chain of events and there will then usually be a last straw in response to which the employee resigns. There can be a cumulative effect of the employer's conduct over a period of time, which gradually breaks down the relationship of trust and confidence (see *Abbey National plc* v. *Robinson* [2001] Emp LR 1, EAT).

The employee must make up his mind to accept the employer's breach and resign, either immediately or on notice, soon after the conduct complained of. If he continues in employment without accepting the breach as terminating the contract for any length of time, without leaving or giving notice, he will be regarded as having elected to affirm the contract.

Remedies

An employee who resigns and claims that he has been constructively dismissed will usually bring two types of claim:

1. A claim for breach of contract.
2. A claim for unfair dismissal, subject to the employee's having the necessary period of qualifying service.

9.5 DAMAGES FOR THE MANNER OF DISMISSAL

An employer's potential liability for damages for unfair dismissal and breach of contract arising out of the dismissal of an employee has been examined in **Chapter 8**. As explained in that chapter, damages for breach of contract are usually assessed on the basis of the salary and benefits the employee would have received had he been given due notice under his contract of employment.

Although under the Employment Rights Act 1996, an employee may also be entitled to compensation in respect of the unfairness of his dismissal, there has historically been no right to recover compensation in a breach of contract claim for the manner in which the dismissal was effected, such as damages for the humiliation and stigma caused by the manner of the dismissal, or the loss of the employee's reputation due to the employer's conduct.

However, over the years the concept of the implied duty of trust and confidence has developed and, in *Malik* v. *Bank Credit and*

Commerce International SA [1997] IRLR 462, the House of Lords held that a breach of the implied duty of trust and confidence could, in certain circumstances, give rise to a claim for damages for loss of reputation caused by a breach of contract. The employees in this case argued that their past association with the disgraced bank placed them at a serious disadvantage in finding new jobs and it was held that, in theory, such loss should be recoverable.

This issue was revisited by the House of Lords in *Johnson v. Unisys Limited* [2001] ICR 480, in which an employee claimed damages in common law for the mental distress he had suffered following his summary dismissal for gross misconduct. The House of Lords refused to allow the employee to pursue his claim on two grounds. The first was on the basis that the implied term of trust and confidence is concerned with preserving the continuing relationship which should subsist between employer and employee and it is not appropriate to use it in connection with the way in which the relationship is terminated. The second ground was that Parliament had provided a limited remedy for just the kind of conduct that the employee was complaining about, i.e. a claim for unfair dismissal.

This approach was followed by the Court of Appeal in *Eastwood & Williams v. Magnox Electric plc* [2002] IRLR 447, in which it was held that it was clear that a claim related to unfairness in the manner of dismissal should be dealt with by the Employment Tribunals and not by way of a common-law action founded in contract or tort.

However, a breach of the implied duty of trust and confidence which is not connected to a dismissal may give rise to a claim of damages for the personal injury caused by that breach of contract.

In *Gogay v. Hertfordshire County Council* [2000] IRLR 703, a residential careworker was suspended following allegations of sexual abuse made by one of the children in her care. An investigation subsequently concluded that there was no case to answer and Ms Gogay was reinstated. However, she was unable to return to work due to clinical depression brought on by her suspension. The Court of Appeal upheld a decision to award Ms Gogay damages in respect of the psychiatric illness caused by her employer's suspending her in breach of the implied term of trust and confidence, which was an action clearly calculated to seriously damage the relationship between the employer and employee.

Similarly, in *McCabe v. Cornwall County Council* [2003] IRLR 87, the Court of Appeal held that the High Court had erred in striking out, as disclosing no cause of action, Mr McCabe's claim for damages for psychiatric injury, allegedly caused by his suspension for four months following allegations of improper conduct, even though he was subsequently dismissed. Mr McCabe's claim was allowed to proceed on the basis that the test was whether the wrongful conduct of the employer formed part of the process of dismissal and that the essential question of fact in any particular case is where the line should be drawn between dismissal, to which a statutory remedy applies, and conduct prior to dismissal causing injury, which can be compensated for in damages at common law.

9.6 PERMANENT HEALTH INSURANCE

It is becoming increasingly common for employers to provide their employees with permanent health insurance as part of their package of contractual benefits. Such schemes provide a form of income protection if the employee is prevented from carrying out his duties beyond a particular period of time due to illness or injury. A typical example would be a scheme providing an employee with 75 per cent of his contractual salary after a 26-week deferred period.

Benefits under such schemes can be particularly valuable, lasting until the employee recovers, he dies, or he reaches normal retirement age. Often, contributions into the employee's pension scheme are also protected.

Disputes can arise under permanent health insurance schemes in a variety of ways. The schemes are often very narrowly drafted, only allowing for benefits to be paid if the employee is not only incapacitated from carrying out his own duties, but also from carrying out any other duties which it might be reasonable for him to assume. Whether the medical evidence supports a claim under such a scheme can also give rise to a debate with the insurers, particularly when dealing with a mental illness rather than a physical one.

If the terms of the contract of employment define the benefit more generously than the terms of the scheme, then an employer can find itself being contractually obliged to pay benefits to an employee that it cannot then recover from the insurer. Careful drafting of employment contracts is therefore essential, preferably giving the employer the right to change the insurance provider or the type of scheme provided from time to time, as it considers appropriate.

The receipt of benefits under a permanent health insurance scheme is usually dependent on the continued employment of the employee by the employer. If the employment contract is terminated, then the benefits will normally cease.

In *Aspden* v. *Webbs Poultry & Meat Group (Holdings) Limited* [1996] IRLR 521, the High Court held that where an employer provides an employee with the benefit of a permanent health insurance scheme, it is an implied term of the contract of employment that, save for in circumstances justifying summary dismissal, the employer will not terminate the contract of employment whilst the employee was incapacitated to work on the grounds of that incapacity, as the employee has a vested right to receive payments under the permanent health insurance scheme.

In such cases, if the employer terminates the contract of employment, thereby depriving the employee of benefits under the permanent health insurance scheme, compensation for breach of contract could also include loss of the benefits the employee would have received under the scheme had it not been for the dismissal. In the case of an employee incapacitated due to a stress-related illness which is likely to last for some time, possibly years, the compensation awarded could be substantial.

9.7 WORKING TIME REGULATIONS 1998

The Working Time Regulations 1998 ('the Regulations') were introduced to implement into UK Law the EU Directive on the Organisation of Working Time (93/104/EC), which is a health and safety measure designed to encourage improvements in the working environment. Certain aspects of the Regulations can be enforced by the Health and Safety Executive, but workers can also bring Employment Tribunal claims under the Regulations and can rely on an employer's breach of the Regulations as evidence to support other types of stress-related claims.

The Regulations set out maximum working hours and minimum rest periods and the main provisions are as follows:

1. Regulation 4 provides that a worker's working time should not exceed an average of 48 hours in any 7-day period. The average is normally calculated over a 17-week reference period. Workers can opt out of the 48-hour week and agree to work longer hours, should they so wish. This opt out is due to be reviewed by the European Council this year and there have been calls for the ability to opt out of the maximum working week to be removed.
2. Regulation 6 provides that a nightworker's normal hours of work in any reference period should not exceed an average of

8 hours in any 24-hour period. Where the work involves special hazards, a worker cannot work more than 8 hours in any 24-hour period and averages cannot be used. Nightworkers also have the right to be offered a free health assessment before being assigned to night work and at regular intervals thereafter.

3. Regulation 10 provides that workers are entitled to a rest period of at least 11 consecutive hours in each 24-hour period.

4. Regulation 11 provides that workers are entitled to a 24-hour uninterrupted rest period in each 7-day period.

5. Regulation 12 provides that if a worker's working day is more than 6 hours long, he is entitled to a 20-minute rest break.

6. Regulation 13 provides that workers are entitled to 4 weeks' paid annual leave. The entitlement to this leave continues to accrue, even when the employee is absent from work due to illness (see *Kigass Aero Components Limited* v. *Brown* [2002] ICR 697, EAT).

There are various exceptions to and derogations from the Regulations for certain categories of workers and certain types of activities. Some of the provisions can also be modified by workforce or collective agreements. There are also special provisions relating to young workers.

Clearly, requiring employees to work excessive hours and/or not providing them with adequate rest periods can affect their health, particularly their mental health. Employees suffering from stress-related illness may bring claims against their employers under the Regulations in the Employment Tribunals and may also use the Regulations to bolster other claims, such as for constructive dismissal or personal injury claims.

9.8 CONCLUSION

Stress and stress-related illnesses can impact on the employment relationship in a number of different ways and it is necessary to think laterally and imaginatively to try to ensure that all types of liabilities are avoided.

CHAPTER 10

Good practice in managing stress

10.1 INTRODUCTION

It is clear that there are a number of different legal requirements which dictate an employer's responsibilities and an employee's rights in relation to workplace stress.

Apart from the legal implications, excessive stress in the workplace can give rise to a number of operational concerns from a business's point of view. Whilst the legal position can appear to be something of a minefield for an employer, some of the principles which emerge can be adapted to enable the employer to develop a practical strategy for managing stress in the workplace which, in addition to providing the basis for a defence to any legal claim, can also assist in ensuring good management practices generally.

The aim of this chapter is to draw together some of the practical guidance and suggest a possible approach to assist an employer in developing an effective stress management strategy. The essence of such a strategy should be to provide a framework in which both proactive and reactive steps for managing stress can be taken. There is still some degree of controversy about the extent to which an employer is under any obligation to proactively manage workplace stress, but the reality of the situation is that without such an approach, an employer is almost inevitably going to find it more difficult to identify genuine problems affecting an individual employee at a sufficiently early stage to do anything about them, as well as to take appropriate action where there is insufficient evidence of a genuine problem.

The framework suggested for a suitable stress management strategy is as follows:

1. Identify whether workplace stress is a relevant risk area for the business in question.

2. Assess the extent of the risk it poses to employees in the business.
3. Devise and develop appropriate steps to monitor individual employees' exposure to workplace stress and to suggest appropriate immediate action.
4. Develop steps to enable an employer to decide how best to deal with an employee who has developed stress-related symptoms.

10.2 IDENTIFYING WHETHER STRESS IS A RELEVANT RISK

As indicated in **Chapter 5**, there are both informal and more formal ways in which levels of stress in the workplace can be identified. For many businesses, the starting point should be to make enquiries of their employees. This could be through the form of a short written questionnaire asking employees to identify any areas of their job or working conditions which cause them particular problems and any which they feel are well managed in the workplace.

It will probably be necessary to introduce the questionnaire as part of an overall project, focusing on this contentious area. Unless employees fully understand the reasons why they are being asked the questions, there is a risk that either the responses will not be accurate or complete, or that many will not participate because of concerns as to the use to which the information will be put, or the purposes for which it is obtained. An individual or a team should be set up to lead the project and that individual or team should begin the process by explaining to employees the process that is about to be undertaken and its aims and objectives.

In addition to the responses of employees to a specific questionnaire on the subject, an employer may be able to gain useful information from considering any or all of the following:

1. Any complaints and/or grievances which appear to relate to workplace stress. These should be monitored to identify any underlying trends.
2. Any ill health records which contain symptoms that may be stress-related, particularly if there is evidence of high levels of sickness absence in a certain team or department, which may indicate that there is an underlying stress issue.
3. Any information obtained through the appraisal or other evaluation process. Employees should be encouraged to raise and discuss any problems they are experiencing through these processes.

The information obtained from these sources may reveal certain anomalies when compared with the responses to the questionnaire. For example, it has been noted elsewhere in this publication that workplace stress is as much a matter of perception as objectively quantifiable fact. An employer may find that when employees are asked direct questions, their answers suggest that their working conditions are stressful, but that there is no previous evidence of any complaint to this effect. This may be because the difficulties the employees are experiencing were not considered sufficiently serious in themselves to warrant a particular complaint or even to warrant mention in the appraisal process. Once the employer indicates an intention to focus on the subject, employees may be more forthcoming.

Alternatively, the absence of any complaints and/or previous concerns about workplace stress may be because employees did not perceive the employer as being receptive to such issues. It is submitted that even in the absence of any prior reason to suspect that workplace stress was an issue, an employer should take its employees' perceptions of the subject seriously. Potentially, the most significant developments in this field will, in the near future, be under the health and safety legislation where the relevant test is not whether any individual employee can in fact demonstrate that he has been made ill by his work, but rather whether it was foreseeable that workplace stress was a relevant risk factor. In addition, the perception by a particular employee that he is stressed may affect how productively and effectively that individual is working and the taking of steps to manage and address the problem could lead to performance-related improvements.

10.3 ASSESSING THE EXTENT OF RISK TO A BUSINESS

In **Chapter 5**, more detailed guidance is given as to the issues that should be considered whilst carrying out a formal risk assessment. In practical terms, the response by employees to the questionnaire referred to above and the employer's own enquiries will have gone someway to identifying:

- what aspects of the employees' working conditions are perceived to be most stressful;
- whether there are universal factors which affect all employees, or more specific factors which only affect parts of the business or certain employees;

- whether the action which has been taken to date by the employer has been sufficient to address these satisfactorily;
- whether there are any improvements which employees themselves suggest.

Employers should, however, be wary of exclusive reliance on what employees themselves report. There may be evidence that particular areas or aspects of the business are stressful to employees, even if none of them specifically refers to them. This may be the case where the cause of the complaint is management style or a cultural issue within the workplace where employees may be reluctant to risk making overt complaints. To some extent, this problem should have been addressed at the outset of the project by explaining to employees that no adverse consequences would arise from their contribution to the investigation and might also be addressed by, for example, anonomysing the questionnaires. However, some reluctance may nevertheless remain and employers should consider whether there is any objective evidence that another aspect of employees' working lives is particularly stressful.

10.4 TAKING APPROPRIATE ACTION

Proactive steps

By the conclusion of the stages identified above, the employer should have a better idea of the action it needs to take to address the risks as they affect its particular business. It is likely that some or all of the following measures will be necessary:

1. Setting up suitable policies and procedures so that individuals can alert management to their particular problems and appropriate action can be taken.
2. Training for managers and employees.
3. Provision of more specialist services, such as occupational health or counselling.

Some of these issues are explored in greater detail below.

Policies and procedures

Workplace stress is an area which may be relevant in the context of a number of different policies and procedures. The business may decide it requires a specific stress management policy. Further information about this is provided in **Chapter 5**. However, in essence, the aim of such a policy should be to set out the business's aims and objectives in terms of stress management, identify individuals with responsibilities for assisting employees who are suffering from stress-related problems, outline the arrangements the business has in place for dealing with workplace stress as an issue and outline the way in which the business intends to monitor the effectiveness of the policy.

Another key policy is likely to be a bullying and harassment policy and further guidance on this can be found in **Chapter 7**. Again, the policy's aims and objectives should be clearly stated and employees should be encouraged to report any problems, so that they can be addressed at an early stage, before they get out of hand and start affecting the employee's health.

Other, more general policies may also be relevant to the management of stress in the workplace. Relevant policies include the business's grievance policy, any policy relating to the management of sickness absence, any capability policy and perhaps even the disciplinary policy. It is not only important to have such policies in place, but employers should also ensure that their employees are aware of the policies and are confident that they will be used effectively. Employees will feel more able to raise concerns if they know that the employer will take them seriously and deal with them appropriately.

Efforts should be made to ensure that these policies of more general application are also adapted in light of the employer's assessment as to the prevalence of workplace stress. When dealing with stress-related issues, a more compassionate and sensitive approach is usually more appropriate.

Training

As with all such projects, there is a risk that the project to devise a stress management strategy may simply generate a new layer of bureaucracy, or toothless policy statements. To avoid this, appropriate training should be given both to managers and to other employees about their roles and responsibilities in the management of workplace stress.

For managers, training can be vital to ensure that, first, they understand the extent of their obligations and, secondly, to help them develop the necessary skills to manage stressed employees effectively. If, for example, the employer decides that there should be an onus on managers to look out for signs of stress amongst employees within their division or department, it is important that the manager knows what the signs of stress are and knows what to do once they have been spotted. Some managers may be reluctant to take on this responsibility. There may be arguments that they are not medically qualified to make the judgments which are necessary. It is therefore vital that their responsibilities are properly and suitably defined and they are given guidance on how to implement the responsibilities in practice. To do otherwise could generate significant amounts of stress at managerial level.

Inevitably, a good deal of the responsibility for spotting signs of stress and alerting management to them will have to fall on the employees themselves. Stress awareness training will arm them with the information they need to identify the signs at an early stage when a relatively simple action should avert a more negative outcome. It may also enable other employees to spot the problem signs and report them to management, even if the employee in question is oblivious of them.

Allied to stress awareness training should be a programme of bullying and harassment awareness. This will help to facilitate the environment necessary for bullying and harassment not to take place and, at the very least, will enable cases of bullying and harassment to be tackled early.

Implementing a stress management strategy

This is a key stage in the overall process. There may be a number of issues which need to be explained to employees. There may have been suggestions and/or requests that cannot be complied with and good communication will ensure that employees are not left feeling that they have not been properly consulted or that their views have not been taken on board at management level. Timescales will also need to be explained. A good stress management strategy may require a fundamental change in the culture in the organisation and this cannot be achieved overnight. Again, if employees are kept informed of the likely timescales involved, then they are less likely to become disgruntled at what they perceive to be any lack of progress.

Monitoring and review

The aim of effective monitoring of the stress management strategy should be to ensure that the steps deemed necessary are in fact being implemented by management and employees. There should also be some way of evaluating the success of the measures implemented. The appraisal system can play a valuable role in this process. If managers have been given specific responsibilities for tackling workplace stress in their departments and divisions, then their performance against the expected outcomes should be raised and assessed at appraisal in the same way as their performance against other targets set by the employer are evaluated. Employers may wish to implement a system whereby levels of stress in the workplace are routinely raised during employee appraisals also.

Reactive measures

In addition to the proactive measures outlined above, employers should give consideration to the way in which they intend to deal with any employee who develops stress-related symptoms or a stress-related illness. Where appropriate, these measures should include provisions for:

1. Obtaining expert medical evidence, whether from the employee's own doctor, an occupational health specialist, or an expert instructed specifically for this purpose (for further details, see **Chapter 8**).
2. Consultation with the employee is usually key to establishing the nature of the illness, its effects, the prognosis and any steps that can be taken to alleviate workplace stress. Only once the employer has this information will it be able to decide how best to proceed.
3. Managing the reaction of other employees, where special arrangements have to be made to give a stressed employee lighter duties or to make adjustments to working arrangements for them.
4. Having an effective and suitable response to complaints/ grievances based on stress-related concerns.
5. Having a system in place to monitor the effectiveness of any individual stress management strategies developed for a particular employee.

10.5 CONCLUSION

Workplace stress can involve a number of complex issues and can be raised in a number of different ways. The key to dealing with it in practice can be summed up in two words: good management.

APPENDIX 1

Sex Discrimination Act 1975
[*as amended*]

PART I
DISCRIMINATION TO WHICH ACT APPLIES

1   Direct and indirect discrimination against women

(1)   In any circumstances relevant for the purposes of any provision of this Act, other than a provision to which subsection (2) applies, a person discriminates against a woman if –

    (a)   on the ground of her sex he treats her less favourably than he treats or would treat a man, or

    (b)   he applies to her a requirement or condition which he applies or would apply equally to a man but –

        (i)   which is such that the proportion of women who can comply with it is considerably smaller than the proportion of men who can comply with it, and

        (ii)   which he cannot show to be justifiable irrespective of the sex of the person to whom it is applied, and

        (iii)   which is to her detriment because she cannot comply with it.

(2)   In any circumstances relevant for the purposes of a provision to which this subsection applies, a person discriminates against a woman if –

    (a)   on the ground of her sex, he treats her less favourably than he treats or would treat a man, or

    (b)   he applies to her a provision, criterion or practice which he applies or would apply equally to a man but –

        (i)   which is such that it would be to the detriment of a considerably larger proportion of women than men, and

        (ii)   which he cannot show to be justifiable irrespective of the sex of the person to whom it is applied, and

        (iii)   which is to her detriment.

(3)   Subsection (2) applies to –

   (a)   any provision of Part 2,
   (b)   sections 35A and 35B, and
   (c)   any other provision of Part 3, so far as it applies to vocational training.

(4)   If a person treats or would treat a man differently according to the man's marital status, his treatment of a woman is for the purposes of subsection (1)(a) or (2)(a) to be compared to his treatment of a man having the same marital status.

2   Sex discrimination against men

(1)   Section 1, and the provisions of Parts II and III relating to sex discrimination against women, are to be read as applying equally to the treatment of men, and for that purpose shall have no effect with such modifications as are requisite.

(2)   In the application of subsection (1) no account shall be taken of special treatment afforded to women in connection with pregnancy or childbirth.

2A   Discrimination on the grounds of gender reassignment

(1)   A person ('A') discriminates against another person ('B') in any circumstances relevant for the purposes of –

   (a)   any provision of Part II,
   (b)   section 35A or 35B, or
   (c)   any other provision of Part III, so far as it applies to vocational training,

   if he treats B less favourably than he treats or would treat other persons, and does so on the ground that B intends to undergo, is undergoing or has undergone gender reassignment.

(2)   Subsection (3) applies to arrangements made by any person in relation to another's absence from work or from vocational training.

(3)   For the purposes of subsection (1), B is treated less favourably than others under such arrangements if, in the application of the arrangements to any absence due to B undergoing gender reassignment –

   (a)   he is treated less favourably than he would be if the absence was due to sickness or injury, or
   (b)   he is treated less favourably than he would be if the absence was due to some other cause and, having regard to the circumstances of the case, it is reasonable for him to be treated no less favourably.

(4) In subsections (2) and (3) 'arrangements' includes terms and conditions or arrangements on which employment, a pupillage or tenancy or vocational training is offered.

(5) For the purposes of subsection (1), a provision mentioned in that subsection framed with reference to discrimination against women shall be treated as applying equally to the treatment of men with such modifications as are requisite.

3 *Direct and indirect discrimination against married persons in employment field*

(1) In any circumstances relevant for the purposes of any provision of Part 2, a person discriminates against a married person of either sex if –

    (a) on the ground of his or her marital status he treats that person less favourably than he treats or would treat an unmarried person of the same sex, or

    (b) he applies to that person a provision, criterion or practice which he applies or would apply equally to an unmarried person, but –

        (i) which is such that it would be to the detriment of a considerably larger proportion of married persons than of unmarried persons of the same sex, and

        (ii) which he cannot show to be justifiable irrespective of the marital status of the person to whom it is applied, and

        (iii) which is to that person's detriment.

(2) For the purposes of subsection (1), a provision of Part 2 framed with reference to discrimination against women shall be treated as applying equally to the treatment of men, and for that purpose shall have effect with such modifications as are requisite.

4 *Discrimination by way of victimisation*

(1) A person ('the discriminator') discriminates against another person ('the person victimised') in any circumstances relevant for the purposes of any provision of this Act if he treats the person victimised less favourably than in those circumstances he treats or would treat other persons, and does so by reason that the person victimised has –

    (a) brought proceedings against the discriminator or any other person under this Act or the Equal Pay Act 1970 or sections 62 to 65 of the Pensions Act 1995, or

    (b) given evidence or information in connection with proceedings brought by any person against the discriminator or any other person under this Act or the Equal Pay Act 1970 or sections 62 to 65 of the Pensions Act 1995, or

(c) otherwise done anything under or by reference to this Act or the Equal Pay Act 1970 or sections 62 to 65 of the Pensions Act 1995 in relation to the discriminator or any other person, or

(d) alleged that the discriminator or any other person has committed an act which (whether or not the allegation so states) would amount to a contravention of this Act or give rise to a claim under the Equal Pay Act 1970 or under sections 62 to 65 of the Pensions Act 1995,

or by reason that the discriminator knows the person victimised intends to do any of those things, or suspects the person victimised has done or intends to do, any of them.

(2) Subsection (1) does not apply to treatment of a person by reason of any allegation made by him if the allegation was false and not made in good faith.

(3) For the purposes of subsection (1), a provision of Part I and II framed with reference to discrimination against women shall be treated as applying equally to the treatment of men and for that purpose shall have effect with such modifications as are requisite.

5 *Interpretation*

(1) In this Act –

(a) references to discrimination refer to any discrimination falling within sections 1 to 4; and

(b) references to sex discrimination refer to any discrimination falling within sections 1 or 2,

and related expressions shall be construed accordingly.

(2) In this Act –

'woman' includes a female of any age, and
'man' includes a male of any age.

(3) A comparison of the cases of persons of different sex or marital status under sections 1(1) or (2) or 3(1), or a comparison of the cases of persons required for the purposes of section 2A, must be such that the relevant circumstances in the one case are the same, or not materially different, in the other.

PART II
DISCRIMINATION IN THE EMPLOYMENT FIELD

DISCRIMINATION BY EMPLOYERS

6 *Discrimination against applicants and employees*

(1) It is unlawful for a person, in relation to employment by him at an establishment in Great Britain, to discriminate against a woman –

    (a) in the arrangements he makes for the purpose of determining who should be offered that employment, or

    (b) in the terms on which he offers her that employment, or

    (c) by refusing or deliberately omitting to offer her that employment.

(2) It is unlawful for a person, in the case of a woman employed by him at an establishment in Great Britain, to discriminate against her –

    (a) in the way he affords her access to opportunities for promotion, transfer or training, or to any other benefits, facilities or services, or by refusing or deliberately omitting to afford her access to them, or

    (b) by dismissing her, or subjecting her to any other detriment.

(3) [*Repealed.*]

(4) Subsections (1)(b) and (2) do not render it unlawful for a person to discriminate against a woman in relation to her membership of, or rights under, an occupational pension scheme in such a way that, were any term of the scheme to provide for discrimination in that way, then, by reason only of any provision made by or under sections 62 to 64 of the Pensions Act 1995 (equal treatment), an equal treatment rule would not operate in relation to that term.

(4A) In subsection (4), 'occupational pension scheme' has the same meaning as in the Pension Schemes Act 1993 and 'equal treatment rule' has the meaning given by section 62 of the Pensions Act 1995.

(5) Subject to section 8(3), subsection (1)(b) does not apply to any provision for the payment of money which, if the woman in question were given the employment, would be included (directly or otherwise) in the contract under which she was employed.

(6) Subsection (2) does not apply to benefits consisting of the payment of money when the provision of those benefits is regulated by the woman's contract of employment.

(7) Subsection (2) does not apply to benefits, facilities or services of any description if the employer is concerned with the provision (for payment or not) of benefits, facilities or services of that

description to the public, or to a section of the public comprising the woman in question, unless –

  (a) that provision differs in a material respect from the provision of the benefits, facilities and services by the employer to his employees, or
  (b) the provision of the benefits, facilities or services to the woman in question is regulated by her contract of employment, or
  (c) the benefits, facilities or services relate to training.

(8) In its application to any discrimination falling within section 2A, this section shall have effect with the omission of subsections (4) to (6).

7 *Exception where sex is a genuine occupational qualification*

  (1) In relation to sex discrimination –

    (a) section 6(1)(a) or (c) does not apply to any employment where being a man is a genuine occupational qualification for the job, and
    (b) section 6(2)(a) does not apply to opportunities for promotion or transfer to, or training for, such employment.

  (2) Being a man is a genuine occupational qualification for a job only where –

    (a) the essential nature of the job calls for a man for reasons of physiology (excluding physical strength or stamina) or, in dramatic performances or other entertainment, for reasons of authenticity, so that the essential nature of the job would be materially different if carried out by a woman, or
    (b) the job needs to be held by a man to preserve decency or privacy because –

      (i) it is likely to involve physical contact with men in circumstances where they might reasonably object to its being carried out by a woman, or
      (ii) the holder of a job is likely to do his work in circumstances where men might reasonably object to the presence of a woman because they are in a state of undress or are using sanitary facilities, or

    (ba) the job is likely to involve the holder of the job doing his work, or living, in a private home and needs to be held by a man because objection might reasonably be taken to allowing to a woman –

124

(i)   the degree of physical or social contact with a person living in the home, or

(ii) the knowledge of intimate details of such a person's life,

which is likely, because of the nature or circumstances of the job or of the home, to be allowed to, or available to, the holder of the job; or

(c) the nature or location of the establishment makes it impracticable for the holder of the job to live elsewhere than in premises provided by the employer, and –

(i)   the only such premises which are available for persons holding that kind of job are lived in, or normally lived in, by men and are not equipped with separate sleeping accommodation for women and sanitary facilities which could be used by women in privacy from men, and

(ii) it is not reasonable to expect the employer either to equip those premises with such accommodation and facilities or to provide premises for women; or

(d) the nature of the establishment, or of the part of it within which the work is done, requires the job to be held by a man because –

(i)   it is, or is part of, a hospital, prison or other establishment for persons requiring special care, supervision or attention, and

(ii)   those persons are all men (disregarding any woman whose presence is exceptional), and

(iii) it is reasonable, having regard to the essential character of the establishment or that part, that the job should not be held be a woman; or

(e) the holder of the job provides individuals with personal services promoting their welfare or education, or similar personal services, and those services can most effectively be provided by a man, or

(f) (*Repealed.*)

(g) the job needs to be held by a man because it is likely to involve the performance of duties outside the United Kingdom in a country whose laws or customs are such that the duties could not, or could not effectively, be performed by a woman, or

(h) the job is one of two to be held by a married couple.

(3) Subsection (2) applies where some only of the duties of the job fall within paragraphs (a) to (g) as well as where all of them do.

(4) Paragraph (a), (b), (c), (d), (e) or (g) of subsection (2) does not apply in relation to the filling of a vacancy at a time when the employer already has male employees –

    (a) who are capable of carrying out the duties falling within that paragraph, and

    (b) whom it would be reasonable to employ on those duties and

    (c) whose numbers are sufficient to meet the employer's likely requirements in respect of those duties without undue inconvenience.

7A   Corresponding exception relating to gender reassignment

(1) In their application to discrimination falling within section 2A, subsections (1) and (2) of section 6 do not make lawful an employer's treatment of another person if –

    (a) in relation to the employment in question –

        (i) being a man is a genuine occupational qualification for the job, or

        (ii) being a woman is a genuine occupational qualification for the job, and

    (b) the employer can show that the treatment is reasonable in view of the circumstances described in the relevant paragraph of section 7(2) and any other relevant circumstances.

(2) In subsection (1) the reference to the employment in question is a reference –

    (a) in relation to any paragraph of section 6(1), to the employment mentioned in that paragraph;

    (b) in relation to section 6(2) –

        (i) in its application to opportunities for promotion or transfer to any employment or for training for any employment, to that employment;

        (ii) otherwise, to the employment in which the person discriminated against is employed or from which that person is dismissed.

(3) In determining for the purposes of subsection (1) whether being a man or being a woman is a genuine occupational qualification for a job, section 7(4) applies in relation to dismissal from employment as it applies in relation to the filling of a vacancy.

7B   Supplementary exceptions relating to gender reassignment

(1)   In relation to discrimination falling within section 2A –

    (a)   section 6(1)(a) or (c) does not apply to any employment where there is a supplementary genuine occupational qualification for the job,

    (b)   section 6(2)(a) does not apply to a refusal or deliberate omission to afford access to opportunities for promotion or transfer to or training for such employment, and

    (c)   section 6(2)(b) does not apply to dismissing an employee from, or otherwise not allowing him to continue in, such employment.

(2)   Subject to subsection (3), there is a supplementary genuine occupational qualification for a job only if –

    (a)   the job involves the holder of the job being liable to be called upon to perform intimate physical searches pursuant to statutory powers;

    (b)   the job is likely to involve the holder of the job doing his work, or living, in a private home and needs to be held otherwise than by a person who is undergoing or has undergone gender reassignment, because objection might reasonably be taken to allowing to such a person –

        (i)   the degree of physical or social contact with a person living in the home, or

        (ii)   the knowledge of intimate details of such a person's life, which is likely, because of the nature or circumstances of the job or of the home, to be allowed to, or available to, the holder of the job;

    (c)   the nature or location of the establishment makes it impracticable for the holder of the job to live elsewhere than in premises provided by the employer, and –

        (i)   the only such premises which are available for persons holding that kind of job are such that reasonable objection could be taken, for the purpose of preserving decency and privacy, to the holder of the job sharing accommodation and facilities with either sex whilst undergoing gender reassignment, and

        (ii)   it is not reasonable to expect the employer either to equip those premises with suitable accommodation or to make alternative arrangements; or

    (d)   the holder of the job provides vulnerable individuals with personal services promoting their welfare, or similar personal services, and in the reasonable view of the employer those services cannot be effectively provided by a person whilst that person is undergoing gender reassignment.

(3) Paragraphs (c) and (d) of subsection (2) apply only in relation to discrimination against a person who –

    (a) intends to undergo gender reassignment, or

    (b) is undergoing gender reassignment.

8   *Equal Pay Act 1970*

(1) [*Amending clause.*]

(2) Section 1(1) of the Equal Pay Act 1970 (as set out in subsection (1) above) does not apply in determining for the purposes of section 6(1)(b) of this Act the terms on which employment is offered.

(3) Where a person offers a woman employment on certain terms, and if she accepted the offer then, by virtue of an equality clause, any of those terms would fall to be modified, or any additional term would fall to be included, the offer shall be taken to contravene section 6(1)(b).

(4) Where a person offers a woman employment on certain terms, and subsection (3) would apply but for the fact that, on her acceptance of the offer, section 1(3) of the Equal Pay Act 1970 (as set out in subsection (1) above) would prevent the equality clause from operating, the offer shall be taken not to contravene section 6(1)(b).

(5) An act does not contravene section 6(2) if –

    (a) it contravenes a term modified or included by virtue of an equality clause, or

    (b) it would contravene such a term but for the fact that the equality clause is prevented from operating by section 1(3) of the Equal Pay Act 1970.

(6) The Equal Pay Act 1970 is further amended as specified in Part I of Schedule 1, and accordingly has effect as set out on Part II of Schedule 1.

(7) In its application to any discrimination falling within section 2A, this section shall have effect with the omission of subsections (3), (4) and (5)(b).

9   *Discrimination against contract workers*

(1) This section applies to any work for a person ('the principal') which is available for doing by individuals ('contract workers') who are employed not by the principal himself but by another person, who supplies them under a contract made with the principal.

(2) It is unlawful for the principal, in relation to work to which this section applies, to discriminate against a woman who is a contract worker –

(a) in the terms on which he allows her to do that work, or

(b) by not allowing her to do it, or

(c) in the way he affords her access to any benefits, facilities or services or by refusing or deliberately omitting to afford her access to them, or

(d) by subjecting her to any other detriment.

(3) Subject to subsection (3A), the principal does not contravene subsection (2)(b) by doing any act in relation to a woman at a time when if the work were to be done by a person taken into his employment being a man would be a genuine occupational qualification for the job.

(3A) Subsection (3) does not apply in relation to discrimination falling within section 2A.

(3B) In relation to discrimination falling within section 2A, the principal does not contravene subsection (2)(a), (b), (c) or (d) by doing any act in relation to a woman if –

(a) he does it at a time when, if the work were to be done by a person taken into his employment –

(i) being a man would be a genuine occupational qualification for the job, or

(ii) being a woman would be a genuine occupational qualification for the job, and

(b) he can show that the act is reasonable in view of the circumstances relevant for the purposes of paragraph (a) and any other relevant circumstances.

(3C) In relation to discrimination falling within section 2A, the principal does not contravene subsection (2)(b) by doing any act in relation to a woman at a time when, if the work were to be done by a person taken into his employment, there would be a supplementary genuine occupational qualification for the job.

(4) Subsection (2)(c) does not apply to benefits, facilities or services of any description if the principal is concerned with the provision (for payment or not) of benefits, facilities or services of that description to the public, or to a section of the public to which the woman belongs, unless that provision differs in a material respect from the provision of the benefits, facilities or services by the principal to his contract workers.

10   Meaning of employment at establishment in Great Britain

(1)   For the purposes of this Part and section 1 of the Equal Pay Act 1970 ('the relevant purposes'), employment is to be regarded as being at an establishment in Great Britain unless the employee does his work wholly outside Great Britain.

(2)   The reference to 'employment' in subsection (1) includes –

(a)   employment on board a ship registered at a port of registry in Great Britain, and

(b)   employment on aircraft or hovercraft registered in the United Kingdom and operated by a person who has his principal place of business, or is ordinarily resident, in Great Britain.

(3)   In the case of employment on board a ship registered at a port of registry in Great Britain (except where the employee does his work wholly outside Great Britain, and outside any area added under subsection (5)) the ship shall for the relevant purposes be deemed to be the establishment.

(4)   Where work is not done at an establishment it shall be treated for the relevant purposes as done at the establishment from which it is done or (where it is not done from any establishment) at the establishment with which it has the closest connection.

(5)   In relation to employment concerned with *exploration of the sea bed or subsoil or the exploitation of their natural resources*, Her Majesty may by Order in Council provide that subsections (1) and (2) shall each have effect as if the last reference to Great Britain included any area for the time being designated under section 1(7) of the Continental Shelf Act 1964, except an area or part of an area in which the law of Northern Ireland applies.

(6)   An Order in Council under subsection (5) may provide that, in relation to employment to which the Order applies, this Part and section 1 of the Equal Pay Act 1970 are to have effect with such modifications as are specified in the Order.

(7)   An Order in Council under subsection (5) shall be of no effect unless a draft Order was laid before and approved by each House of Parliament.

[. . .]

41   Liability of employers and principals

(1)   Anything done by a person in the course of his employment shall be treated for the purposes of this Act as done by his employer as well as by him, whether or not it was done with the employer's knowledge or approval.

(2) Anything done by a person as agent for another person with the authority (whether express or implied, and whether precedent or subsequent) of that other person shall be treated for the purposes of this Act as done by that other person as well as by him.

(3) In proceedings brought under this Act against any person in respect of an act alleged to have been done by an employee of his it shall be defence for that person to prove that he took such steps as were reasonably practicable to prevent the employee from doing that act, or from doing in the course of his employment acts of that description.

[. . .]

Race Relations Act 1976
[*as amended*]

PART I
DISCRIMINATION TO WHICH ACT APPLIES

1 Racial discrimination

(1) A person discriminates against another in any circumstances relevant for the purposes of any provision of this Act if –

    (a) on racial grounds he treats that other less favourably than he treats or would treat other persons; or

    (b) he applies to that other a requirement or condition which he applies or would apply equally to persons not of the same racial group as that other but –

        (i) which is such that the proportion of persons of the same racial group as that other who can comply with it is considerably smaller than the proportion of persons not of that racial group who can comply with it; and

        (ii) which he cannot show to be justifiable irrespective of the colour, race, nationality or ethnic or national origins of the person to whom it is applied; and

        (iii) which is to the detriment of that other because he cannot comply with it.

(2) It is hereby declared that, for the purposes of this Act, segregating a person from other persons on racial grounds is treating him less favourably than they are treated.

2 Discrimination by way of victimisation

(1) A person ('the discriminator') discriminates against another person ('the person victimised') in any circumstances relevant for the purposes of any provision of this Act if he treats the person victimised less favourably than in those circumstances he treats or would treat other persons, and does so by reason that the person victimised has –

    (a)   brought proceedings against the discriminator or any other person under this Act; or

    (b)   given evidence or information in connection with proceedings brought by any person against the discriminator or any other person under this Act; or

    (c)   otherwise done anything under or by reference to this Act in relation to the discriminator or any other person; or

    (d)   alleged that the discriminator or any other person has committed an act which (whether or not the allegation so states) would amount to a contravention of this Act,

or by reason that the discriminator knows that the person victimised intends to do any of these things, or suspects that the person victimised has done, or intends to do, any of them.

(2)   Subsection (1) does not apply to treatment of a person by reason of any allegation made by him if the allegation was false and not made in good faith.

3   *Meaning of 'racial grounds', 'racial groups', etc.*

(1)   In this Act, unless the context otherwise requires –

'racial grounds' means any of the following grounds, namely colour, race, nationality or ethnic or national origins;

'racial group; means a group of persons defined by reference to colour, race, nationality or ethnic or national origins, and reference to a person's racial group refer to any racial group into which he falls.

(2)   The fact that a racial group comprises two or more distinct racial groups does not prevent it from constituting a particular racial group for the purposes of this Act.

(3)   In this Act –

    (a)   references to discrimination refer to any discrimination falling within section 1 or 2; and

    (b)   references to racial discrimination refer to any discrimination falling within section 1,

and related expressions shall be construed accordingly.

(4)   A comparison of the case of a person of a particular racial group with that of a person not of that group under section 1(1) must be such that the relevant circumstances in the one case are the same, or not materially different, in the other.

3A. *Harassment*

(1)   A person subjects another to harassment in any circumstances relevant for the purposes of any provision referred to in section 1(1B)

where, on grounds of race or ethnic or national origins, he engages in unwanted conduct which has the purpose or effect of –

(a) violating that other person's dignity; or
(b) creating an intimidating, hostile, degrading, humiliating or offensive environment for him.

(2) Conduct shall be regarded as having the effect specified in paragraph (a) or (b) of subsection (1) only if, having regard to all the circumstances, including in particular the perception of that other person, it should reasonably be considered as having that effect.

PART II
DISCRIMINATION IN THE EMPLOYMENT FIELD

DISCRIMINATION BY EMPLOYERS

4 Discrimination against applicants and employees

(1) It is unlawful for a person, in relation to employment by him at an establishment in Great Britain, to discriminate against another –

(a) in the arrangements he makes for the purpose of determining who should be offered that employment;
(b) in terms on which he offers him that employment; or
(c) by refusing or deliberately omitting to offer him that employment.

(2) It is unlawful for a person, in the case of a person employed by him at an establishment in Great Britain, to discriminate against that employee –

(a) in the terms of employment which he affords him; or
(b) in the way he affords him access to opportunities for promotion, transfer or training, or to any other benefits, facilities or services, or by refusing or deliberately omitting to afford him access to them; or
(c) by dismissing him, or subjecting him to any other detriment.

(3) Except in relation to discrimination falling within section 2, subsections (1) and (2) do not apply for employment for the purposes of a private household.

(4) Subsection (2) does not apply to benefits, facilities or services of any description if the employer is concerned with the provision (for payment or not) of benefits, facilities or services of that description to the public, or to a section of the public comprising the employee in question, unless –

(a) that provision differs in a material respect from the provision of the benefits, facilities or services by the employer to his employees; or

(b) the provision of the benefits, facilities or services to the employee in question is regulated by his contract of employment; or

(c) the benefits, facilities or services relate to training.

5 *Exceptions for genuine occupational qualifications*

(1) In relation to racial discrimination –

(a) section 4(1)(a) or (c) does not apply to any employment where being of a particular racial group is a genuine occupational qualification for the job; and

(b) section 4(2)(b) does not apply to opportunities for promotion or transfer to, or training for, such employment.

(2) Being of a particular racial group is a genuine occupational qualification for a job only where –

(a) the job involves participation in a dramatic performance or other entertainment in a capacity for which a person of that racial group is required for reasons of authenticity; or

(b) the job involves participation as an artist's or photographic model in the production of a work of art, visual image or sequence of visual images for which a person of that racial group is required for reasons of authenticity; or

(c) the job involves working in a place where food or drink is (for payment or not) provided to and consumed by members of the public or a section of the public in a particular setting for which, in that job, a person of that racial group is required for reasons of authenticity; or

(d) the holder of the job provides persons of that racial group with personal services promoting their welfare, and those services can most effectively be provided by a person of that racial group.

(3) Subsection (2) applies where some only of the duties of the job fall within paragraph (a), (b), (c) or (d) as well as where all of them do.

(4) Paragraph (a), (b), (c) or (d) of subsection (2) does not apply in relation to the filling of a vacancy at a time when the employer already has employees of the racial group in question –

(a) who are capable of carrying out the duties falling within that paragraph; and

(b) whom it would be reasonable to employ on those duties; and

(c) whose numbers are sufficient to meet the employer's likely requirements in respect of those duties without undue inconvenience.

6 *Exception for employment intended to provide training in skills to be exercised outside Great Britain*

Nothing in section 4 shall render unlawful any act done by an employer for the benefit of a person not ordinarily resident in Great Britain in or in connection with employing him at an establishment in Great Britain, where the purpose of that employment is to provide him with training in skills which he appears to the employer to intend to exercise wholly outside Great Britain.

7 *Discrimination against contract workers*

(1) This section applies to any work for a person ('the principal') which is available for doing by individuals ('contract workers') who are employed not by the principal himself but by another person, who supplies them under a contract made with the principal.

(2) It is unlawful for the principal, in relation to work to which this section applies, to discriminate against a contract worker –

    (a) in the terms on which he allows him to do that work; or

    (b) by not allowing him to do it or continue to do it; or

    (c) in the way he affords him access to any benefits, facilities or services or by refusing or deliberately omitting to afford him access to them; or

    (d) by subjecting him to any other detriment.

(3) The principal does not contravene subsection (2)(b) by doing any act in relation to a person not of a particular racial group at a time when, if the work were to be done by a person taken into the principal's employment, being of that racial group would be a genuine occupational qualification for the job.

(4) Nothing in this section shall render unlawful any act done by the principal for the benefit of a contract worker not ordinarily resident in Great Britain in or in connection with allowing him to do work to which this section applies, where the purpose of his being allowed to do that work is to provide him with training skills which he appears to the principal to intend to exercise wholly outside Great Britain.

(5) Subsection (2)(c) does not apply to benefits, facilities or services of any description if the principal is concerned with the provision (for payment or not) of benefits, facilities or services of that description to the public, or to a section of the public to which the contract worker in question belongs, unless that provision differs in a material respect from the provision of the benefits, facilities or services by the principal to his contract workers.

8   Meaning of employment at establishment in Great Britain

    (1)   For the purposes of this Part ('the relevant purposes'), employment is to be regarded as being at an establishment in Great Britain unless the employee does his work wholly outside Great Britain.

    (2)   (*Repealed.*)

    (3)   In the case of employment on board a ship registered at a port of registry in Great Britain (except where the employee does his work wholly outside Great Britain) the ship shall for the relevant purposes be deemed to be the establishment.

    (4)   Where work is not done at an establishment it shall be treated for the relevant purposes as done at the establishment from which it is done or (where it is not done from any establishment) at the establishment with which it has the closest connection.

    (5)   In relation to employment concerned with exploration of the sea bed or subsoil or the exploitation of their natural resources, Her Majesty may by Order in Council provide that subsections (1) and subsection (3) the last reference to Great Britain included any area for the time being designated under section 1(7) of the Continental Shelf Act 1964, except an area or part of an area in which the law of Northern Ireland applies.

    (6)   An Order in Council under subsection (5) may provide that, in relation to the employment to which the Order applies, this Part is to have effect with such modifications as are specified in the Order.

    (7)   An Order in Council under subsection (5) shall be of no effect unless a draft of the Order has been laid before and approved by resolution of each House of Parliament.

[. . .]

32   Liability of employers and principals

    (1)   Anything done by a person in the course of his employment shall be treated for the purposes of this Act (except as regards offences thereunder) as done by his employer as well as by him, whether or not it was done with the employer's knowledge or approval.

    (2)   Anything done by a person as agent for another person with the authority (whether express or implied, and whether precedent or subsequent) of that other person shall be treated for the purposes of this Act (except as regards offences thereunder) as done by that other person as well as by him.

    (3)   In proceedings brought under this Act against any person in respect of an act alleged to have been done by an employee of his it shall be a defence for that person to prove that he took such steps as were reasonably practicable to prevent the employee from doing that act, or from doing in the course of his employment acts of that description.

Disability Discrimination Act 1995

PART I
DISABILITY

1 Meaning of 'disability' and 'disabled person'

(1) Subject to the provisions of Schedule 1, a person has a disability for the purposes of this Act if he has a physical or mental impairment which has a substantial and long-term adverse effect on his ability to carry out normal day-to-day activities.

(2) In this Act 'disabled person' means a person who has a disability.

2 Past disabilities

(1) The provisions of this Part and Parts II and III apply in relation to a person who has had a disability as they apply in relation to a person who has that disability.

(2) Those provisions are subject to the modifications made by Schedule 2.

(3) Any regulations or order made under this Act may include provision with respect to persons who have had a disability.

(4) In any proceedings under Part II or Part III of this Act, the question whether a person had a disability at a particular time ('the relevant time') shall be determined, for the purposes of this section, as if the provisions of, or made under, this Act in force when the act complained of was done had been in force at the relevant time.

(5) The relevant time may be a time before the passing of this Act.

3 Guidance

(1) The Secretary of State may issue guidance about the matters to be taken into account in determining –

(a) whether an impairment has a substantial adverse effect on a person's ability to carry out normal day-to-day activities; or

(b) whether such an impairment has a long-term effect.

(2) The guidance may, among other things, give examples of –

(a) effects which it would be reasonable, in relation to particular activities, to regard for purposes of this Act as substantial adverse effects;

(b) effects which it would not be reasonable, in relation to particular activities, to regard for such purposes as substantial adverse effects;

(c) substantial adverse effects which it would be reasonable to regard, for such purposes, as long-term;

(d) substantial adverse effects which it would not be reasonable to regard, for such purposes, as long-term.

(3) A tribunal or court determining, for any purpose of this Act, whether an impairment has a substantial and long-term adverse effect on a person's ability to carry out normal day-to-day activities, shall take into account any guidance which appears to it to be relevant.

(4) In preparing a draft of any guidance, the Secretary of State shall consult such persons as he considers appropriate.

(5) Where the Secretary of State proposes to issue any guidance, he shall publish a draft of it, consider any representations that are made to him about the draft and, if he thinks it appropriate, modify his proposals in the light of any of those representations.

(6) If the Secretary of State decides to proceed with any proposed guidance, he shall lay a draft of it before each House of Parliament.

(7) If, within the 40-day period, either House resolves not to approve the draft, the Secretary of State shall take no further steps in relation to the proposed guidance.

(8) If no such resolution is made within the 40-day period, the Secretary of State shall issue the guidance in the form of his draft.

(9) The guidance shall come into force on such date as the Secretary of State may appoint by order.

(10) Subsection (7) does not prevent a new draft of the proposed guidance from being laid before Parliament.

(11) The Secretary of State may –

(a) from time to time revise the whole or part of any guidance and re-issue it;

(b) by order revoke any guidance.

(12) In this section –

'40-day period', in relation to the draft of any proposed guidance, means –

(a) if the draft is laid before one House on a day later than the day on which it is laid before the other House, the period of 40 days beginning with the later of the two days, and

(b) in any other case, the period of 40 days beginning with the day on which the draft is laid before each House,

no account being taken of any period during which Parliament is dissolved or prorogued or during which both Houses are adjourned for more than 4 days; and

'guidance' means guidance issued by the Secretary of State under this section and includes guidance which has been revised and re-issued.

Part II
Employment

DISCRIMINATION BY EMPLOYERS

4   Discrimination against applicants and employees

(1) It is unlawful for an employer to discriminate against a disabled person –

(a) in the arrangements which he makes for the purpose of determining to whom he should offer employment;

(b) in the terms on which he offers that person employment; or

(c) by refusing to offer, or deliberately not offering, him employment.

(2) It is unlawful for an employer to discriminate against a disabled person whom he employs –

(a) in the terms of employment which he affords him;

(b) in the opportunities which he affords him for promotion, a transfer, training or receiving any other benefit;

(c) by refusing to afford him, or deliberately not affording him, any such opportunity; or

(d) by dismissing him, or subjecting him to any other detriment.

(3) Subsection (2) does not apply to benefits of any description if the employer is concerned with the provision (whether or not for payment) of benefits of that description to the public, or to a section of the public which includes the employee in question, unless –

(a) that provision differs in a material respect from the provision of the benefits by the employer to his employees; or

(b) the provision of the benefits to the employee in question is regulated by his contract of employment; or

(c) the benefits relate to training.

(4) In this Part 'benefits' includes facilities and services.

(5) In the case of an act which constitutes discrimination by virtue of section 55, this section also applies to discrimination against a person who is not disabled.

(6) This section applies only in relation to employment at an establishment in Great Britain.

5 *Meaning of 'discrimination'*

(1) For the purposes of this Part, an employer discriminates against a disabled person if –

(a) for a reason which relates to the disabled person's disability, he treats him less favourably than he treats or would treat others to whom that reason does not or would not apply; and

(b) he cannot show that the treatment in question is justified.

(2) For the purposes of this Part, an employer also discriminates against a disabled person if –

(a) he fails to comply with a section 6 duty imposed on him in relation to the disabled person; and

(b) he cannot show that his failure to comply with that duty is justified.

(3) Subject to subsection (5), for the purposes of subsection (1) treatment is justified if, but only if, the reason for it is both material to the circumstances of the particular case and substantial.

(4) For the purposes of subsection (2), failure to comply with a section 6 duty is justified if, but only if, the reason for the failure is both material to the circumstances of the particular case and substantial.

(5) If, in a case falling within subsection (1), the employer is under a section 6 duty in relation to the disabled person but fails without justification to comply with that duty, his treatment of that person cannot be justified under subsection (3) unless it would have been justified even if he had complied with the section 6 duty.

(6) Regulations may make provision, for purposes of this section, as to circumstances in which –

(a) treatment is to be taken to be justified;

(b) failure to comply with a section 6 duty is to be taken to be justified;

    (c)   treatment is to be taken not to be justified;
    (d)   failure to comply with a section 6 duty is to be taken not to be justified.

(7)   Regulations under subsection (6) may, in particular –

    (a)   make provision by reference to the cost of affording any benefit; and
    (b)   in relation to benefits under occupational pension schemes, make provision with a view to enabling uniform rates of contributions to be maintained.

6 *Duty of employer to make adjustments*

(1)   Where –

    (a)   any arrangements made by or on behalf of an employer, or
    (b)   any physical feature of premises occupied by the employer,

place the disabled person concerned at a substantial disadvantage in comparison with persons who are not disabled, it is the duty of the employer to take such steps as it is reasonable, in all the circumstances of the case, for him to have to take in order to prevent the arrangements or feature having that effect.

(2)   Subsection (1)(a) applies only in relation to –

    (a)   arrangements for determining to whom employment should be offered;
    (b)   any term, condition or arrangements on which employment, promotion, a transfer, training or any other benefit is offered or afforded.

(3)   The following are examples of steps which an employer may have to take in relation to a disabled person in order to comply with subsection (1) –

    (a)   making adjustments to premises;
    (b)   allocating some of the disabled person's duties to another person;
    (c)   transferring him to fill an existing vacancy;
    (d)   altering his working hours;
    (e)   assigning him to a different place of work;
    (f)   allowing him to be absent during working hours for rehabilitation, assessment or treatment;
    (g)   giving him, or arranging for him to be given, training;
    (h)   acquiring or modifying equipment;
    (i)   modifying instructions or reference manuals;
    (j)   modifying procedures for testing or assessment;
    (k)   providing a reader or interpreter;
    (l)   providing supervision.

(4)   In determining whether it is reasonable for an employer to have to take a particular step in order to comply with subsection (1), regard shall be had, in particular, to –

    (a)   the extent to which taking the step would prevent the effect in question;

    (b)   the extent to which it is practicable for the employer to take the step;

    (c)   the financial and other costs which would be incurred by the employer in taking the step and the extent to which taking it would disrupt any of his activities;

    (d)   the extent of the employer's financial and other resources;

    (e)   the availability to the employer of financial or other assistance with respect to taking the step.

This subsection is subject to any provision of regulations made under subsection (8).

(5)   In this section, 'the disabled person concerned' means –

    (a)   in the case of arrangements for determining to whom employment should be offered, any disabled person who is, or has notified the employer that he may be, an applicant for that employment;

    (b)   in any other case, a disabled person who is –

        (i)   an applicant for the employment concerned; or

        (ii)   an employee of the employer concerned.

(6)   Nothing in this section imposes any duty on an employer in relation to a disabled person if the employer does not know, and could not reasonably be expected to know –

    (a)   in the case of an applicant or potential applicant, that the disabled person concerned is, or may be, an applicant for the employment; or

    (b)   in any case, that that person has a disability and is likely to be affected in the way mentioned in subsection (1).

(7)   Subject to the provisions of this section, nothing in this Part is to be taken to require an employer to treat a disabled person more favourably than he treats or would treat others.

(8)   Regulations may make provision, for the purposes of subsection (1) –

    (a)   as to circumstances in which arrangements are, or a physical feature is, to be taken to have the effect mentioned in that subsection;

    (b)   as to circumstances in which arrangements are not, or a physical feature is not, to be taken to have that effect;

(c) as to circumstances in which it is reasonable for an employer to have to take steps of a prescribed description;

(d) as to steps which it is always reasonable for an employer to have to take;

(e) as to circumstances in which it is not reasonable for an employer to have to take steps of a prescribed description;

(f) as to steps which it is never reasonable for an employer to have to take;

(g) as to things which are to be treated as physical features;

(h) as to things which are not to be treated as such features.

(9) Regulations made under subsection (8)(c), (d), (e) or (f) may, in particular, make provision by reference to the cost of taking the steps concerned.

(10) Regulations may make provision adding to the duty imposed on employers by this section, including provision of a kind which may be made under subsection (8).

(11) This section does not apply in relation to any benefit under an occupational pension scheme or any other benefit payable in money or money's worth under a scheme or arrangement for the benefit of employees in respect of –

(a) termination of service;

(b) retirement, old age or death;

(c) accident, injury, sickness or invalidity; or

(d) any other prescribed matter.

(12) This section imposes duties only for the purpose of determining whether an employer has discriminated against a disabled person; and accordingly a breach of any such duty is not actionable as such.

[. . .]

ENFORCEMENT ETC.

8 *Enforcement, remedies and procedure*

(1) A complaint by any person that another person –

(a) has discriminated against him in a way which is unlawful under this Part, or

(b) is, by virtue of section 57 or 58, to be treated as having discriminated against him in such a way,

may be presented to an employment tribunal.

(2) Where an employment tribunal finds that a complaint presented to it under this section is well-founded, it shall take such of the following steps as it considers just and equitable –

(a) making a declaration as to the rights of the complainant and the respondent in relation to the matters to which the complaint relates;

(b) ordering the respondent to pay compensation to the complainant;

(c) recommending that the respondent take, within a specified period, action appearing to the tribunal to be reasonable, in all the circumstances of the case, for the purpose of obviating or reducing the adverse effect on the complainant of any matter to which the complaint relates.

(3) Where a tribunal orders compensation under subsection (2)(b), the amount of the compensation shall be calculated by applying the principles applicable to the calculation of damages in claims in tort or (in Scotland) in reparation for breach of statutory duty.

(4) For the avoidance of doubt it is hereby declared that compensation in respect of discrimination in a way which is unlawful under this Part may include compensation for injury to feelings whether or not it includes compensation under any other head.

(5) If the respondent to a complaint fails, without reasonable justification, to comply with a recommendation made by an employment tribunal under subsection (2)(c) the tribunal may, if it thinks it just and equitable to do so –

(a) increase the amount of compensation required to be paid to the complainant in respect of the complaint, where an order was made under subsection (2)(b); or

(b) make an order under subsection (2)(b).

(6) Regulations may make provision –

(a) for enabling a tribunal, where an amount of compensation falls to be awarded under subsection (2)(b), to include in the award interest on that amount; and

(b) specifying, for cases where a tribunal decides that an award is to include an amount in respect of interest, the manner in which and the periods and rate by reference to which the interest is to be determined.

(7) Regulations may modify the operation of any order made under section 14 of the Employment Tribunals Act 1996 (power to make provision as to interest on sums payable in pursuance of industrial tribunal decisions) to the extent that it relates to an award of compensation under subsection (2)(b).

(8) Part I of Schedule 3 makes further provision about the enforcement of this Part and about procedure.

[. . .]

58   Liability of employers and principals

(1)   Anything done by a person in the course of his employment shall be treated for the purposes of this Act as also done by his employer, whether or not it was done with the employer's knowledge or approval.

(2)   Anything done by a person as agent for another person with the authority of that other person shall be treated for the purposes of this Act as also done by that other person.

(3)   Subsection (2) applies whether the authority was –

(a)   express or implied; or

(b)   given before or after the act in question was done.

(4)   Subsections (1) and (2) do not apply in relation to an offence under section 57(4).

(5)   In proceedings under this Act against any person in respect of an act alleged to have been done by an employee of his, it shall be a defence for that person to prove that he took such steps as were reasonably practicable to prevent the employee from –

(a)   doing that act; or

(b)   doing, in the course of his employment, acts of that description.

[. . .]

SCHEDULE 1
Provisions Supplementing Section 1

IMPAIRMENT

1.– (1) 'Mental impairment' includes an impairment resulting from or consisting of a mental illness only if the illness is a clinically well-recognised illness.

(2)   Regulations may make provision, for the purposes of this Act –

(a)   for conditions of a prescribed description to be treated as amounting to impairments;

(b)   for conditions of a prescribed description to be treated as not amounting to impairments.

(3)   Regulations made under sub-paragraph (2) may make provision as to the meaning of 'condition' for the purposes of those regulations.

LONG-TERM EFFECTS

2.– (1) The effect of an impairment is a long-term effect if –

    (a)   it has lasted at least 12 months;

    (b)   the period for which it lasts is likely to be at least 12 months; or

    (c)   it is likely to last for the rest of the life of the person affected.

    (3)   Where an impairment ceases to have a substantial adverse effect on a person's ability to carry out normal day-to-day activities, it is to be treated as continuing to have that effect if that effect is likely to recur.

    (4)   For the purposes of sub-paragraph (2), the likelihood of an effect recurring shall be disregarded in prescribed circumstances.

    (4)   Regulations may prescribe circumstances in which, for the purposes of this Act –

    (a)   an effect which would not otherwise be a long-term effect is to be treated as such an effect; or

    (b)   an effect which would otherwise be a long-term effect is to be treated as not being such an effect.

SEVERE DISFIGUREMENT

3.– (1) An impairment which consists of a severe disfigurement is to be treated as having a substantial adverse effect on the ability of the person concerned to carry out normal day-to-day activities.

    (2)   Regulations may provide that in prescribed circumstances a severe disfigurement is not to be treated as having that effect.

    (3)   Regulations under sub-paragraph (2) may, in particular, make provision with respect to deliberately acquired disfigurements.

NORMAL DAY-TO-DAY ACTIVITIES

4.– (1) An impairment is to be taken to affect the ability of the person concerned to carry out normal day-to-day activities only if it affects one of the following –

    (a)   mobility;

    (b)   manual dexterity;

    (c)   physical co-ordination;

    (d)   continence;

    (e)   ability to lift, carry or otherwise move everyday objects;

    (f)   speech, hearing or eyesight;

    (g)   memory or ability to concentrate, learn or understand; or

    (h)   perception of the risk of physical danger.

    (2)   Regulations may prescribe –

    (a)   circumstances in which an impairment which does not have an effect falling within sub-paragraph (1) is to be taken to affect the ability of the person concerned to carry out normal day-to-day activities;

    (b)   circumstances in which an impairment which has an effect falling within sub-paragraph (1) is to be taken not to affect the ability of the person concerned to carry out normal day-to-day activities.

SUBSTANTIAL ADVERSE EFFECTS

5.– Regulations may make provision for the purposes of this Act –

    (a)   for an effect of a prescribed kind on the ability of a person to carry out normal day-to-day activities to be treated as a substantial adverse effect;

    (b)   for an effect of a prescribed kind on the ability of a person to carry out normal day-to-day activities to be treated as not being a substantial adverse effect.

EFFECT OF MEDICAL TREATMENT

6.– (1) An impairment which would be likely to have a substantial adverse effect on the ability of the person concerned to carry out normal day-to-day activities, but for the fact that measures are being taken to treat or correct it, is to be treated as having that effect.

(2)   In sub-paragraph (1) 'measures' includes, in particular, medical treatment and the use of a prosthesis or other aid.

(3)   Sub-paragraph (1) does not apply –

    (a)   in relation to the impairment of a person's sight, to the extent that the impairment is, in his case, correctable by spectacles or contact lenses or in such other ways as may be prescribed; or

    (b)   in relation to such other impairments as may be prescribed, in such circumstances as may be prescribed.

PERSONS DEEMED TO BE DISABLED

7.– (1) Sub-paragraph (2) applies to any person whose name is, both on 12th January 1995 and on the date when this paragraph comes into force, in the register of disabled persons maintained under section 6 of the Disabled Persons (Employment) Act 1944.

(2)   That person is to be deemed –

    (a)   during the initial period, to have a disability, and hence to be a disabled person; and

   (b)   afterwards, to have had a disability and hence to have been a disabled person during that period.

(3)   A certificate of registration shall be conclusive evidence, in relation to the person with respect to whom it was issued, of the matters certified.

(4)   Unless the contrary is shown, any document purporting to be a certificate of registration shall be taken to be such a certificate and to have been validly issued.

(5)   Regulations may provide for prescribed descriptions of person to be deemed to have disabilities, and hence to be disabled persons, for the purposes of this Act.

(6)   Regulations may prescribe circumstances in which a person who has been deemed to be a disabled person by the provisions of sub-paragraph (1) or regulations made under sub-paragraph (5) is to be treated as no longer being deemed to be such a person.

(7)   In this paragraph –

'certificate of registration' means a certificate issued under regulations made under section 6 of the Act of 1944; and
'initial period' means the period of three years beginning with the date on which this paragraph comes into force.

PROGRESSIVE CONDITIONS
8.– (1)   Where –

   (a)   a person has a progressive condition (such as cancer, multiple sclerosis or muscular dystrophy or infection by the human immunodeficiency virus),
   (b)   as a result of that condition, he has an impairment which has (or had) an effect on his ability to carry out normal day-to-day activities, but
   (c)   that effect is not (or was not) a substantial adverse effect,

he shall be taken to have an impairment which has such a substantial adverse effect if the condition is likely to result in his having such an impairment.

(2)   Regulations may make provision, for the purposes of this paragraph –

   (a)   for conditions of a prescribed description to be treated as being progressive;
   (b)   for conditions of a prescribed description to be treated as not being progressive.

[. . .]

Employment Rights Act 1996

[. . .]

86   Rights of employer and employee to minimum notice

(1)   The notice required to be given by an employer to terminate the contract of employment of a person who has been continuously employed for one month or more –

(a)   is not less than one week's notice if his period of continuous employment is less than two years,

(b)   is not less than one week's notice for each year of continuous employment if his period of continuous employment is two years or more but less than twelve years, and

(c)   is not less than twelve weeks' notice if his period of continuous employment is twelve years or more.

(2)   The notice required to be given by an employee who has been continuously employed for one month or more to terminate his contract of employment is not less than one week.

(3)   Any provision for shorter notice in any contract of employment with a person who has been continuously employed for one month or more has effect subject to subsections (1) and (2); but this section does not prevent either party from waiving his right to notice on any occasion or from accepting a payment in lieu of notice.

(4)   Any contract of employment of a person who has been continuously employed for three months or more which is a contract for a term certain of one month or less shall have effect as if it were for an indefinite period; and, accordingly, subsections (1) and (2) apply to the contract.

(5)   (*Repealed.*)

(6)   This section does not affect any right of either party to a contract of employment to treat the contract as terminable without notice by reason of the conduct of the other party.

87 Rights of employee in period of notice

(1) If an employer gives notice to terminate the contract of employment of a person who has been continuously employed for one
month or more, the provisions of sections 88 to 91 have effect as
respects the liability of the employer for the period of notice
required by section 86(1).

(2) If an employee who has been continuously employed for one
month or more gives notice to terminate his contract of employment, the provisions of sections 88 to 91 have effect as respects the
liability of the employer for the period of notice required by
section 86(2).

(3) In sections 88 to 91 'period of notice' means –

(a) where notice is given by an employer, the period of notice
required by section 86(1), and
(b) where notice is given by an employee, the period of notice
required by section 86(2).

(4) This section does not apply in relation to a notice given by the
employer or the employee if the notice to be given by the employer
to terminate the contract must be at least one week more than the
notice required by section 86(1).

88 Employments with normal working hours

(1) If an employee has normal working hours under the contract of
employment in force during the period of notice and during any
part of those normal working hours –

(a) the employee is ready and willing to work but no work is provided for him by his employer,
(b) the employee is incapable of work because of sickness or
injury,
(c) the employee is absent from work wholly or partly because of
pregnancy or childbirth, or
(d) the employee is absent from work in accordance with the
terms of his employment relating to holidays,

the employer is liable to pay the employee for the part of normal
working hours covered by any of paragraphs (a), (b), (c) and (d) a
sum not less than the amount of remuneration for that part of normal working hours calculated at the average hourly rate of remuneration produced by dividing a week's pay by the number of
normal working hours.

(2) Any payments made to the employee by his employer in respect of
the relevant part of the period of notice (whether by way of sick
pay, statutory sick pay, maternity pay, statutory maternity pay,

holiday pay or otherwise) go towards meeting the employer's liability under this section.

(3) Where notice was given by the employee, the employer's liability under this section does not arise unless and until the employee leaves the service of the employer in pursuance of the notice.

[. . .]

PART X
UNFAIR DISMISSAL

CHAPTER I
RIGHT NOT TO BE UNFAIRLY DISMISSED

THE RIGHT

94   *The right*

(1) An employee has the right not to be unfairly dismissed by his employer.

(2) Subsection (1) has effect subject to the following provisions of this Part (in particular sections 108 to 110) and to the provisions of the Trade Union and Labour Relations (Consolidation) Act 1992 (in particular sections 237 to 239).

DISMISSAL

95   *Circumstances in which an employee is dismissed*

(1) For the purposes of this Part an employee is dismissed by his employer if (and, subject to subsection (2) and section 96, only if) –

(a) the contract under which he is employed is terminated by the employer (whether with or without notice),

(b) he is employed under a limited-term contract and that contract terminates by virtue of the limiting event without being renewed under the same contract, or

(c) the employee terminates the contract under which he is employed (with or without notice) in circumstances in which he is entitled to terminate it without notice by reason of the employer's conduct.

(2) An employee shall be taken to be dismissed by his employer for the purposes of this Part if –

(a) the employer gives notice to the employee to terminate his contract of employment, and

153

(b) at a time within the period of that notice the employee gives notice to the employer to terminate the contract of employment on a date earlier than the date on which the employer's notice is due to expire;

and the reason for the dismissal is to be taken to be the reason for which the employer's notice is given.

[. . .]

FAIRNESS

98 *General*

(1) In determining for the purposes of this Part whether the dismissal of an employee is fair or unfair, it is for the employer to show –

(a) the reason (or, if more than one, the principal reason) for the dismissal, and

(b) that it is either a reason falling within subsection (2) or some other substantial reason of a kind such as to justify the dismissal of an employee holding the position which the employee held.

(2) A reason falls within this subsection if it –

(a) relates to the capability or qualifications of the employee for performing work of the kind which he was employed by the employer to do,

(b) relates to the conduct of the employee,

(c) is that the employee was redundant, or

(d) is that the employee could not continue to work in the position which he held without contravention (either on his part or on that of his employer) of a duty or restriction imposed by or under an enactment.

(3) In subsection (2)(a) –

(a) 'capability', in relation to an employee, means his capability assessed by reference to skill, aptitude, health or any other physical or mental quality, and

(b) 'qualifications', in relation to an employee, means any degree, diploma or other academic, technical or professional qualification relevant to the position which he held.

(4) Where the employer has fulfilled the requirements of subsection (1), the determination of the question whether the dismissal is fair or unfair (having regard to the reason shown by the employer) –

(a) depends on whether in the circumstances (including the size and administrative resources of the employer's undertaking) the employer acted reasonably or unreasonably in treating it as a sufficient reason for dismissing the employee, and

(b) shall be determined in accordance with equity and the substantial merits of the case.

(5) Where the employee is taken to be dismissed for the purposes of this Part by virtue of section 96, subsection (4)(a) applies as if for the words 'acted reasonably' onwards there were substituted the words 'would have been acting reasonably or unreasonably in treating it as a sufficient reason for dismissing the employee if she had not been absent from work, and'.

(6) Subsection (4) is subject to –

(a) sections 98A to 107 of this Act, and

(b) sections 152, 153 and 238 of the Trade Union and Labour Relations (Consolidation) Act 1992 (dismissal on ground of trade union membership or activities or in connection with industrial action).

[. . .]

EXCLUSION OF RIGHT

108 Qualifying period of employment

(1) Section 94 does not apply to the dismissal of an employee unless he has been continuously employed for a period of not less than one year ending with the effective date of termination.

(2) If an employee is dismissed by reason of any such requirement or recommendation as is referred to in section 64(2), subsection (1) has effect in relation to that dismissal as if for the words 'one year' there were substituted the words 'one month'.

(3) Subsection (1) does not apply if –

(a) [*Repealed.*]

(b) subsection (1) of section 99 (read with subsection (2) of that section) or subsection (3) of that section applies,

(c) subsection (1) of section 100 (read with subsections (2) and (3) of that section) applies,

(d) subsection (1) of section 101 (read with subsection (2) of that section) or subsection (3) of that section applies,

(dd) section 101A applies,

(e) section 102 applies,

(f) section 103 applies,

(ff) section 103A applies,

(g) subsection (1) of section 104 (read with subsections (2) and (3) of that section) applies,

(gg) subsection (1) of section 104A (read with subsection (2) of that section) applies,

(gh) subsection 1(1) of subsection 104B (read with subsection (2) of that section) applies,

(h) section 105 applies,

(hh) paragraph (3) or (6) of regulation 28 of the Transnational Information and Consultation of Employees Regulations 1999 (read with paragraphs (4) and (7) of that regulation) applies,

(i) paragraph (1) of regulation (7) of the Part-Time Workers (prevention of Less Favourable Treatment) Regulations 2000 applies, or

(j) paragraph (1) of regulation 6 of the Fixed term Employees (Prevention of Less Favourable treatment) Regulations 2002 applies.

[. . .]

CHAPTER II
REMEDIES FOR UNFAIR DISMISSAL

INTRODUCTORY

111 Complaints to employment tribunal

(1) A complaint may be presented to an employment tribunal against an employer by any person that he was unfairly dismissed by the employer.

(2) Subject to subsection (3), an employment tribunal shall not consider a complaint under this section unless it is presented to the tribunal –

(a) before the end of the period of three months beginning with the effective date of termination, or

(b) within such further period as the tribunal considers reasonable in a case where it is satisfied that it was not reasonably practicable for the complaint to be presented before the end of that period of three months.

(3) Where a dismissal is with notice, an employment tribunal shall consider a complaint under this section if it is presented after the notice is given but before the effective date of termination.

(4) In relation to a complaint which is presented as mentioned in subsection (3), the provisions of this Act, so far as they relate to unfair dismissal, have effect as if –

(a) references to a complaint by a person that he was unfairly dismissed by his employer included references to a complaint by a person that his employer has given him notice in such circumstances that he will be unfairly dismissed when the notice expires,

(b) references to reinstatement included references to the withdrawal of the notice by the employer,

(c) references to the effective date of termination included references to the date which would be the effective date of termination on the expiry of the notice, and

(d) references to an employee ceasing to be employed included references to an employee having been given notice of dismissal.

[. . .]

APPENDIX 5

COMMISSION RECOMMENDATION of 27 November 1991 on the protection of the dignity of women and men at work (92/131/EEC)

THE COMMISSION OF THE EUROPEAN COMMUNITIES,

Having regard to the Treaty establishing the European Economic Community, and in particular the second indent of Article 155 thereof,

Whereas unwanted conduct of a sexual nature, or other conduct based on sex affecting the dignity of women and men at work, including the conduct of superiors and colleagues, is unacceptable and may, in certain circumstances, be contrary to the principle of equal treatment within the meaning of Articles 3, 4 and 5 of Council Directive 76/207/EEC of 9 February 1976 on the implementation of the principle of equal treatment for men and women as regards access to employment, vocational training and promotion, and working conditions, a view supported by case-law in some Member States;

Whereas, in accordance with the Council recommendation of 13 December 1984 on the promotion of positive action for women, many Member States have carried out a variety of positive action measures and actions having a bearing, inter alia, on respect for the dignity of women at the workplace;

Whereas the European Parliament, in its resolution of 11 June 1986 on violence against women, has called upon national governments, equal opportunities committees and trade unions to carry out concerted information campaigns to create a proper awareness of the individual rights of all members of the labour force;

Whereas the Advisory Committee on Equal Opportunities for Women and Men, in its opinion of 20 June 1988, has unanimously recommended that there should be a recommendation and code of conduct on sexual harassment in the workplace covering harassment of both sexes;

Whereas the Commission in its action programme relating to the implementation of the Community Charter of Basic Social Rights for Workers undertook to examine the protection of workers and their dignity at work, having regard to the reports and recommendations prepared on various aspects of implementation of Community law;

Whereas the Council, in its resolution of 29 May 1990 on the protection of the dignity of women and men at work, affirms that conduct based on sex affecting the dignity of women and men at work, including conduct of superiors and colleagues, constitutes an intolerable violation of the dignity of workers or trainees, and calls on the Member States and the institutions and organs of the European Communities to develop positive measures designed to create a climate at work in which women and men respect one another's human integrity;

Whereas the Commission, in its third action programme on equal opportunities for women and men, 1991 to 1995, and pursuant to paragraph 3 of the said Council resolution of 29 May 1990, resolved to draw up a code of conduct on the protection of the dignity of women and men at work, based on experience and best practice in the Member States, to provide guidance on initiating and pursuing positive measures designed to create a climate at work in which women and men respect one another's human integrity;

Whereas the European Parliament, on 22 October 1991, adopted a resolution on the protection of the dignity of women and men at work;

Whereas the Economic and Social Committee, on 30 October 1991, adopted an opinion on the protection of the dignity of women and men at work,

RECOMMENDS AS FOLLOWS:

Article 1

It is recommended that the Member States take action to promote awareness that conduct of a sexual nature, or other conduct based on sex affecting the dignity of women and men at work, including conduct of superiors and colleagues, is unacceptable if:

(a) such conduct is unwanted, unreasonable and offensive to the recipient;

(b) a person's rejection of, or submission to, such conduct on the part of employers or workers (including superiors or colleagues) is used explicitly or implicitly as a basis for a decision which affects that person's access to vocational training, access to employment, continued employment, promotion, salary or any other employment decisions; and/or

(c) such conduct creates an intimidating, hostile or humiliating work environment for the recipient; and that such conduct may, in certain circumstances, be contrary to the principle of equal treatment within the meaning of Articles 3, 4 and 5 of Directive 76/207/EEC.

Article 2

It is recommended that Member States take action, in the public sector, to implement the Commission's code of practice on the protection of the dignity of women and men at work, annexed hereto. The action of the Member States, in thus initiating and pursuing positive measures designed to create a climate at work in which women and men respect one another's human integrity, should serve as an example to the private sector.

Article 3

It is recommended that Member States encourage employers and employee representatives to develop measures to implement the Commission's code of practice on the protection of the dignity of women and men at work.

Article 4

Member States shall inform the Commission within three years of the date of this recommendation of the measures taken to give effect to it, in order to allow the Commission to draw up a report on all such measures. The Commission shall, within this period, ensure the widest possible circulation of the code of practice. The report should examine the degree of awareness of the Code, its perceived effectiveness, its degree of application and the extent of its use in collective bargaining between the social partners.

Article 5

This recommendation is addressed to the Member States. Done at Brussels, 27 November 1991. For the Commission

Vasso Papandreou
Member of the Commission

PROTECTING THE DIGNITY OF WOMEN AND MEN AT WORK
A code of practice on measures to combat sexual harassment

1. INTRODUCTION

This code of practice is issued in accordance with the resolution of the Council of Ministers on the protection of the dignity of women and men at work, and to accompany the Commission's recommendation on this issue.

Its purpose is to give practical guidance to employers, trade unions, and employees on the protection of the dignity of women and men at work. The code is intended to be applicable in both the public and the private sector and employers are encouraged to follow the recommendations contained in the code in a way which is appropriate to the size and structure of their organization. It may be particularly relevant for small and medium-sized enterprises to adapt some of the practical steps to their specific needs.

The aim is to ensure that sexual harassment does not occur and, if it does occur, to ensure that adequate procedures are readily available to deal with the problem and prevent its recurrence. The code thus seeks to encourage the development and implementation of policies and practices which establish

161

working environments free of sexual harassment and in which women and men respect one another's human integrity.

The expert report carried out on behalf of the Commission found that sexual harassment is a serious problem for many working women in the European Community and research in Member States has proven beyond doubt that sexual harassment at work is not an isolated phenomenon. On the contrary, it is clear that for millions of women in the European Community, sexual harassment is an unpleasant and unavoidable part of their working lives. Men too may suffer sexual harassment and should, of course, have the same rights as women to the protection of their dignity.

Some specific groups are particularly vulnerable to sexual harassment. Research in several Member States, which documents the link between the risk of sexual harassment and the recipient's perceived vulnerability, suggests that divorced and separated women, young women and new entrants to the labour market and those with irregular or precarious employment contracts, women in non-traditional jobs, women with disabilities, lesbians and women from racial minorities are disproportionately at risk. Gay men and young men are also vulnerable to harassment. It is undeniable that harassment on grounds of sexual orientation undermines the dignity at work of those affected and it is impossible to regard such harassment as appropriate workplace behaviour.

Sexual harassment pollutes the working environment and can have a devastating effect upon the health, confidence, morale and performance of those affected by it. The anxiety and stress produced by sexual harassment commonly leads to those subjected to it taking time off work due to sickness, being less efficient at work, or leaving their job to seek work elsewhere. Employees often suffer the adverse consequences of the harassment itself and short- and long-term damage to their employment prospects if they are forced to change jobs. Sexual harassment may also have a damaging impact on employees not themselves the object of unwanted behaviour but who are witness to it or have a knowledge of the unwanted behaviour.

There are also adverse consequences arising from sexual harassment for employers. It has a direct impact on the profitability of the enterprise where staff take sick leave or resign their posts because of sexual harassment, and on the economic efficiency of the enterprise where employees' productivity is reduced by having to work in a climate in which individuals' integrity is not respected.

In general terms, sexual harassment is an obstacle to the proper integration of women into the labour market and the Commission is committed to encouraging the development of comprehensive measures to improve such integration.

2. *DEFINITION*

Sexual harassment means unwanted conduct of a sexual nature, or other conduct based on sex affecting the dignity of women and men at work. This can include unwelcome physical, verbal or non-verbal conduct. Thus, a range of behaviour may be considered to constitute sexual harassment. It is unacceptable if such conduct is unwanted, unreasonable and offensive to the recipient; a person's rejection of or submission to such conduct on the part of employers or workers (including superiors or colleagues) is used explicitly or implicitly as a basis for a decision which affects that person's access to vocational training or to employment, continued employment, promotion, salary or any other employment decisions; and/or such conduct creates an intimidating, hostile or humiliating working environment for the recipient.

The essential characteristic of sexual harassment is that it is unwanted by the recipient, that it is for each individual to determine what behaviour is acceptable to them and what they regard as offensive. Sexual attention becomes sexual harassment if it is persisted in once it has been made clear that it is regarded by the recipient as offensive, although one incident of harassment may constitute sexual harassment if sufficiently serious. It is the unwanted nature of the conduct which distinguishes sexual harassment from friendly behaviour, which is welcome and mutual.

3. *THE LAW AND EMPLOYERS' RESPONSIBILITIES*

Conduct of a sexual nature or other based on sex affecting the dignity of women and men at work may be contrary to the principle of equal treatment within the meaning of Articles 3, 4 and 5 of Council Directive 76/207/EEC of 9 February 1976 on the implementation of the principle of equal treatment for men and women as regards access to employment, vocational training and promotion, and working conditions. This principle means that there shall be no discrimination whatsoever on grounds of sex either directly or indirectly by reference in particular to marital or family status.

In certain circumstances, and depending upon national law, sexual harassment may also be a criminal offence or may contravene other obligations imposed by the law, such as health and safety duties, or a duty, contractual or otherwise, to be a good employer. Since sexual harassment is a form of employee misconduct, employers have a responsibility to deal with it as they do with any other form of employee misconduct as well as to refrain from harassing employees themselves. Since sexual harassment is a risk to health and safety, employers have a responsibility to take steps to minimize the risk as they do with other hazards. Since sexual harassment often entails an abuse of power, employers may have a responsibility for the misuse of the authority they delegate.

This code, however, focuses on sexual harassment as a problem of sex discrimination. Sexual harassment is sex discrimination because the gender of the recipient is the determining factor in who is harassed. Conduct of a sexual nature or other conduct based on sex affecting the dignity of women and men at work in some Member States already has been found to contravene national equal treatment laws and employers have a responsibility to seek to ensure that the work environment is free from such conduct.

As sexual harassment is often a function of women's status in the employment hierarchy, policies to deal with sexual harassment are likely to be most effective where they are linked to a broader policy to promote equal opportunities and to improve the position of women. Advice on steps which can be taken generally to implement an equal opportunities policy is set out in the Commission's guide to positive action.

Similarly, a procedure to deal with complaints of sexual harassment should be regarded as only one component of a strategy to deal with the problem. The prime objective should be to change behaviour and attitudes, to seek to ensure the prevention of sexual harassment.

4. COLLECTIVE BARGAINING

The majority of the recommendations contained in this code are for action by employers, since employers have clear responsibilities to ensure the protection of the dignity of women and men at work.

Trade unions also have responsibilities to their members and they can and should play an important role in the prevention of sexual harassment in the workplace. It is recommended that the question of including appropriate clauses in agreements be examined in the context of the collective bargaining process, with the aim of achieving a work environment free from unwanted conduct of a sexual nature or other conduct based on sex affecting the dignity of women and men at work and free from victimization of a complainant or of a person wishing to give, or giving, evidence in the event of a complaint.

5. RECOMMENDATIONS TO EMPLOYERS

The policies and procedures recommended below should be adopted, where appropriate, after consultation or negotiation with trade unions or employee representatives. Experience suggests that strategies to create and maintain a working environment in which the dignity of employees is respected are most likely to be effective where they are jointly agreed.

It should be emphasized that a distinguishing characteristic of sexual harassment is that employees subjected to it often will be reluctant to complain. An absence of complaints about sexual harassment in a particular organization, therefore, does not necessarily mean an absence of sexual harassment. It may mean that the recipients of sexual harassment think that there is no point in complaining because nothing will be done about it, or because it will be trivialized or the complainant subjected to ridicule, or because they fear reprisals. Implementing the preventative and procedural recommendations outlined below should facilitate the creation of a climate at work in which such concerns have no place.

A. Prevention

(i) POLICY STATEMENTS

As a first step in showing senior management's concern and their commitment to dealing with the problem of sexual harassment, employers should issue a policy statement which expressly states that all employees have a right to be treated with dignity, that sexual harassment at work will not be permitted or condoned and that employees have a right to complain about it should it occur.

It is recommended that the policy statement make clear what is considered inappropriate behaviour at work, and explain that such behaviour, in certain circumstances, may be unlawful. It is advisable for the statement to set out a positive duty on managers and supervisors to implement the policy and to take corrective action to ensure compliance with it. It should also place a positive duty on all employees to comply with the policy and to ensure that their colleagues are treated with respect and dignity.

In addition, it is recommended that the statement explain the procedure which should be followed by employees subjected to sexual harassment at work in order to obtain assistance and to whom they should complain; that it contain an undertaking that allegations of sexual harassment will be dealt with seriously, expeditiously and confidentially, and that employees will be protected against victimization or retaliation for bringing a complaint of sexual harassment. It should also specify that appropriate disciplinary measures will be taken against employees found guilty of sexual harassment.

(ii) COMMUNICATING THE POLICY

Once the policy has been developed, it is important to ensure that it is communicated effectively to all employees, so that they are aware that they have a right to complain and to whom they should complain; that their complaint will be dealt with promptly and fairly; and that employees are made aware of the likely consequences of engaging in sexual harassment. Such communication will highlight management's commitment to eliminating sexual harassment, thus enhancing a climate in which it will not occur.

(iii) RESPONSIBILITY

All employees have a responsibility to help to ensure a working environment in which the dignity of employees is respected and managers (including supervisors) have a particular duty to ensure that sexual harassment does not occur in work areas for which they are responsible. It is recommended that managers explain the organization's policy to their staff and take steps to positively promote the policy. Managers should also be responsive and supportive to any member of staff who complains about sexual harassment, provide full and clear advice on the procedure to be adopted, maintain confidentiality in any cases of sexual harassment and ensure that there is no further problem of sexual harassment or any victimization after a complaint has been resolved.

(iv) TRAINING

An important means of ensuring that sexual harassment does not occur and that, if it does occur, the problem is resolved efficiently is through the provision of training for managers and supervisors. Such training should aim to identify the factors which contribute to a working environment free of sexual harassment and to familiarize participants with their responsibilities under the employer's policy and any problems they are likely to encounter.

In addition, those playing an official role in any formal complaints procedure in respect of sexual harassment should receive specialist training, such as that outlined above.

It is also good practice to include information as to the organization's policy on sexual harassment and procedures for dealing with it as part of appropriate induction and training programmes.

B. Procedures

The development of clear and precise procedures to deal with sexual harassment once it has occurred is of great importance. The procedures should ensure the resolution of problems in an efficient and effective manner. Practical guidance for employees on how to deal with sexual harassment when it occurs and with its aftermath will make it more likely that it will be dealt with at an early stage. Such guidance should of course draw attention to an employee's legal rights and to any time limits within which they must be exercised.

(i) RESOLVING PROBLEMS INFORMALLY

Most recipients of harassment simply want the harassment to stop. Both informal and formal methods of resolving problems should be available.

Employees should be advised that, if possible, they should attempt to resolve the problem informally in the first instance. In some cases, it may be possible and sufficient for the employee to explain clearly to the person engaging in the unwanted conduct that the behaviour in question is not welcome, that it offends them or makes them uncomfortable, and that it interferes with their work. In circumstances where it is too difficult or embarrassing for an individual to do this on their own behalf, an alternative approach would be to seek support from, or for an initial approach to be made by, a sympathetic friend or confidential counsellor.

If the conduct continues or if it is not appropriate to resolve the problem informally, it should be raised through the formal complaints procedure.

(ii) ADVICE AND ASSISTANCE

It is recommended that employers designate someone to provide advice and assistance to employees subjected to sexual harassment, where possible with responsibilities to assist in the resolution of any problems, whether through informal or formal means. It may be helpful if the officer is designated with the agreement of the trade unions or employees, as this is likely to enhance their acceptability. Such officers could be selected from personnel departments or equal opportunities departments for example. In some organizations they are designated as 'confidential counsellors' or 'sympathetic friends'. Often such a role may be played by someone from the employee's trade union or women's support groups.

Whatever the location of this responsibility in the organization, it is recommended that the designated officer receives appropriate training in the best means of resolving problems and in the detail of the organization's policy and procedures, so that they can perform their role effectively. It is also important that they are given adequate resources to carry out their function, and protection against victimization for assisting any recipient of sexual harassment.

(iii) COMPLAINTS PROCEDURE

It is recommended that, where the complainant regards attempts at informal resolution as inappropriate, where informal attempts at resolution have been refused, or where the outcome has been unsatisfactory, a formal procedure for resolving the complaint be provided. The procedure should give employees confidence that the organization will take allegations of sexual harassment seriously.

By its nature sexual harassment may make the normal channels of complaint difficult to use because of embarrassment, fears of not being taken seriously, fears of damage to reputation, fears of reprisal or the prospect of damaging the working environment. Therefore, a formal procedure should specify to whom the employee should bring a complaint, and it should also provide an alternative if in the particular circumstances the normal grievance procedure may not be suitable, for example because the alleged harasser is the employee's line manager. It is also advisable to make provision for employees to bring a complaint in the first instance to someone of their own sex, should they so choose.

It is good practice for employers to monitor and review complaints of sexual harassment and how they have been resolved, in order to ensure that their procedures are working effectively.

(iv) INVESTIGATIONS

It is important to ensure that internal investigations of any complaints are handled with sensitivity and with due respect for the rights of both the complainant and the alleged harasser. The investigation should be seen to be independent and objective. Those carrying out the investigation should not be connected with the allegation in any way, and every effort should be made to resolve complaints speedily – grievances should be handled promptly and the procedure should set a time limit within which complaints will be processed, with due regard for any time limits set by national legislation for initiating a complaint through the legal system.

It is recommended as good practice that both the complainant and the alleged harasser have the right to be accompanied and/or represented, perhaps by a representative of their trade union or a friend or colleague; that the alleged harasser be given full details of the nature of the complaint and the opportunity to respond, and that strict confidentiality be maintained throughout any investigation into an allegation. Where it is necessary to interview witnesses, the importance of confidentiality should be emphasized.

It must be recognized that recounting the experience of sexual harassment is difficult and can damage the employee's dignity. Therefore, a complainant should not be required repeatedly to recount the events complained of where this is unnecessary.

The investigation should focus on the facts of the complaint and it is advisable for the employer to keep a complete record of all meetings and investigations.

(v) DISCIPLINARY OFFENCE

It is recommended that violations of the organization's policy protecting the dignity of employees at work should be treated as a disciplinary offence and the disciplinary rules should make clear what is regarded as inappropriate behaviour at work. It is also good practice to ensure that the range of penalties to which offenders will be liable for violating the rule is clearly stated and also to make it clear that it will be considered a disciplinary offence to victimize or retaliate against an employee for bringing a complaint of sexual harassment in good faith.

Where a complaint is upheld and it is determined that it is necessary to relocate or transfer one party, consideration should be given, wherever practicable, to allowing the complainant to choose whether he or she wishes to remain in their post or be transferred to another location. No element of penalty should be seen to attach to a complainant whose complaint is upheld and in addition, where a complaint is upheld, the employer should monitor the situation to ensure that the harassment has stopped.

Even where a complaint is not upheld, for example because the evidence is regarded as inconclusive, consideration should be given to transferring or rescheduling the work of one of the employees concerned rather than requiring them to continue to work together against the wishes of either party.

6. RECOMMENDATIONS TO TRADE UNIONS

Sexual harassment is a trade union issue as well as an issue for employers. It is recommended as good practice that trade unions formulate and issue clear policy statements on sexual harassment and take steps to raise awareness of the problem of sexual harassment in the workplace, in order to help create a climate in which it is neither condoned nor ignored. For example, trade unions could aim to give all officers and representatives training on equality issues, including dealing with sexual harassment, and include such information in union-sponsored or approved training courses, as well as information on the union's policy. Trade unions should consider declaring that sexual harassment is inappropriate behaviour and educating members and officials about its consequences is recommended as good practice.

Trade unions should also raise the issue of sexual harassment with employers and encourage the adoption of adequate policies and procedures to protect the dignity of women and men at work in the organization. It is advisable for trade unions to inform members of their right not to be sexually harassed at work and provide members with clear guidance as to what to do if they are sexually harassed, including guidance on any relevant legal rights.

Where complaints arise, it is important for trade unions to treat them seriously and sympathetically and ensure that the complainant has an opportunity of representation if a complaint is to be pursued. It is important to create an environment in which members feel able to raise such complaints knowing they will receive a sympathetic and supportive response from local union representatives. Trade unions could consider designating specially trained officials to advise and counsel members with complaints of sexual harassment and act on their behalf if required. This will provide a focal point for support. It is also a good idea to ensure that there are sufficient female representatives to support women subjected to sexual harassment.

It is recommended too, where the trade union is representing both the complainant and the alleged harasser for the purpose of the complaints procedure, that it be made clear that the union is not condoning offensive behaviour by providing representation. In any event, the same official should not represent both parties.

It is good practice to advise members that keeping a record of incidents by the harassed worker will assist in bringing any formal or informal action to a more effective conclusion, that the union wishes to be informed of any incident of sexual harassment and that such information will be kept confidential. It is also good practice for the union to monitor and review the union's record in responding to complaints and in representing alleged harassers and the harassed, in order to ensure its responses are effective.

7. EMPLOYEES' RESPONSIBILITIES

Employees have a clear role to play in helping to create a climate at work in which sexual harassment is unacceptable. They can contribute to preventing sexual harassment through an awareness and sensitivity towards the issue and by ensuring that standards of conduct for themselves and for colleagues do not cause offence.

Employees can do much to discourage sexual harassment by making it clear that they find such behaviour unacceptable and by supporting colleagues who suffer such treatment and are considering making a complaint. Employees who are themselves recipients of harassment should, where practicable, tell the harasser that the behaviour is unwanted and unacceptable. Once the offender understands clearly that the behaviour is unwelcome, this may be enough to put an end to it. If the behaviour is persisted in, employees should inform management and/or their employee representative through the appropriate channels and request assistance in stopping the harassment, whether through informal or formal means.

HSE Leaflets

Who is this leaflet for?

You may have seen the guidance book *Tackling work-related stress: A managers' guide to improving and maintaining employee health and well-being*. That guidance is aimed at your manager, who has a duty to ensure your health is not harmed by work-related stress. In particular, he or she must:

● assess the risk to your health from work-related stress;
● put in place measures to eliminate (or where that is not possible, reduce) that risk;
● consult you, either directly or through your trade union (TU) or other representative, about workplace and organisational changes that are likely to significantly affect your health or safety.

This leaflet contains information on what you can do to help your manager.

REMEMBER: stress is not a weakness and you don't have to suffer. Your employer has a duty to protect your health and safety at work and a good employer will appreciate any suggestions you have for reducing work-related stress. Work-related stress is a symptom of an organisational problem, not an individual weakness.

What is work-related stress?

Stress is the adverse reaction people have to excessive pressure or other types of demand placed on them. It can be caused by things at work or by things outside of work, or both. This leaflet is concerned with work-related stress: that is, stress that arises from, or is made worse by, work. Work-related stress is not an illness, but it can lead to increased problems with ill health, if it is prolonged or particularly intense. For example:

● physical effects:
  • heart disease;
  • back pain, gastrointestinal disturbances and various minor illnesses;
● psychological effects:
  • anxiety and depression.

You are not alone if you feel very or extremely stressed. In the country as a whole, as many as one in five people could be feeling the same way. In the workplace, the Management of Health and Safety at Work Regulations 1999 require you as an employee to tell your employer about any shortcomings in their health and safety arrangements. This is particularly important when tackling work-related stress – it requires a partnership between you, your manager, and your employer: a partnership based on honesty and trust, where you all say what you feel.

What can you do at work?

You can help at work by:

- 'doing your bit' for managing work-related stress by talking to your employer: if they don't know there's a problem, they can't help. If you don't feel able to talk directly to your employer or manager, ask a TU or other employee representative to raise the issue on your behalf;
- supporting your colleagues if they are experiencing work-related stress. Encourage them to talk to their manager, TU or staff representative;
- seeing if your employer's counselling or employee assistance service (if provided), can help;
- speaking to your GP if you are worried about your health;
- discussing with your manager whether it is possible to alter your job to make it less stressful for you, recognising your and your colleagues' needs;
- trying to channel your energy into solving the problem rather than just worrying about it. Think about what would make you happier at work and discuss this with your employer.

What can you do out of work?

The following advice will not prevent work-related stress, but may help you take care of yourself and ensure that you don't make the problem worse. You can:

- eat healthily;
- stop smoking – it doesn't help you to stay healthy, even though you might think it relaxes you;
- try to keep within Government recommendations for alcohol consumption – alcohol acts as depressant and will not help you tackle the problem;
- watch your caffeine intake – tea, coffee and some soft drinks (e.g. cola drinks) may contribute to making you feel more anxious;
- be physically active – it stimulates you and gives you more energy;
- try learning relaxation techniques – some people find it helps them cope with pressures in the short term;
- talk to family or friends about what you're feeling – they may be able to help you and provide the support you need to raise your concerns at work.

What to do after a stress-related illness

If you have been off work with a stress-related illness, talk about it with your employer when you return. Say how you feel, explain what led to the event and what you would like to see happen. Take a TU representative or a work colleague with you if you do not feel you can do this on your own.

Further information

Tackling work-related stress: A managers' guide to improving and maintaining employee health and well-being HSG218 2001 HSE Books ISBN 0 7176 2050 6 is available from HSE Books

This leaflet is available in priced packs of 20 from HSE Books, ISBN 0 7176 2065 4. Single free copies are also available from HSE Books.

While every effort has been made to ensure the accuracy of the references listed in this publication, their future availability cannot be guaranteed.

HSE priced and free publications are available by mail order from HSE Books, PO Box 1999, Sudbury, Suffolk CO10 2WA Tel: 01787 881165 Fax: 01787 313995 Website: www.hsebooks.co.uk (HSE priced publications are also available from bookshops.)

For information about health and safety ring HSE's InfoLine Tel: 08701 545500 Fax: 02920 859260 e-mail: hseinformationservices@natbrit.com or write to HSE Information Services, Caerphilly Business Park, Caerphilly CF83 3GG. You can also visit HSE's website: www.hse.gov.uk

This leaflet contains notes on good practice which are not compulsory but which you may find helpful in considering what you need to do.

INDG341   10/01   C4000
Printed and published by the Health and Safety Executive

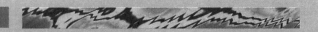

This booklet answers some common questions about work-related stress. It explains what it is, and what you can do about it. The advice is intended specifically for managers of small firms, or organisations employing up to 50 staff. If you employ more than 50 people, you may find our more detailed guide, *Tackling work-related stress: A managers' guide to improving and maintaining employee health and well-being*, more useful. The booklet does not introduce any concepts that are different from good management. Our belief is that plain good management can reduce work-related stress where it is already occurring, and can prevent it in the first place.

Q *What is stress?*

A Stress is the adverse reaction people have to excessive pressure. It isn't a disease. But if stress is intense and goes on for some time, it can lead to mental and physical ill health (eg depression, nervous breakdown, heart disease).

Q *But stress can be a good thing, can't it?*

A No! Being under *pressure* often improves performance. It can be a good thing. But when demands and pressures become excessive, they lead to *stress*. And it's clear from the recognised symptoms of stress that it's actually *bad* for you.

OK -PRESSURES -STRESS -ILL-HEALTH

Q *As an employer, is it my concern?*

A Yes. It's your duty in law to make sure that your employees aren't made ill by their work. And stress *can* make your employees ill. Also, action to reduce stress can be very cost-effective. The costs of stress to your organisation may show up as high staff turnover, an increase in sickness absence, reduced work performance, poor timekeeping and more customer complaints. Stress in one person can also lead to stress in staff who have to cover for their colleague. Also, employers who don't take stress seriously may leave themselves open to compensation claims from employees who have suffered ill health from work-related stress. Fortunately, reducing stress need not cost you a lot of money.

Q *Under health and safety law, what must I do about stress?*

A Where stress caused or made worse by work could lead to ill health, you must assess the risk. A risk assessment for stress involves:

- looking for pressures at work that could cause high and long-lasting levels of stress;
- deciding who might be harmed by these; and
- deciding whether you are doing enough to prevent that harm.

1

If necessary, you must then take reasonable steps to deal with those pressures. You must review the assessment whenever you think that it may no longer be valid. You should make sure that you involve your employees – including Trade Union safety representatives where they have been appointed – at every stage of the assessment process.

Q Isn't stress also caused by problems outside work? Are you saying I have to do something about that?

A You're not under a legal duty to prevent ill health caused by stress due to problems outside work, eg financial or domestic worries. But non-work problems can make it difficult for people to cope with the pressures of work, and their performance at work might suffer. So being understanding to staff in this position would be in your interests.

Q Are some people more likely to suffer from stress than others?

A We're all vulnerable to stress, depending on the pressure we're under at any given time: even people who are usually very hardy. As an employer, you're responsible for making sure that work doesn't make your employees ill. If you notice that someone is particularly vulnerable because of their circumstances, look at how their work is organised. See if there are ways to relieve the pressures so that they do not become excessive. However, unless you know otherwise, you could assume that all your employees are mentally capable of withstanding reasonable pressure from work.

Q How do I recognise stress in a particular person?

A Many of the outward signs of stress in individuals should be noticeable to managers and colleagues. Look in particular for changes in a person's mood or behaviour, such as deteriorating relationships with colleagues, irritability, indecisiveness, absenteeism or reduced performance. Those suffering from stress may also smoke or drink alcohol more than usual or even turn to drugs. They might also complain about their health: for example they may get frequent headaches.

2

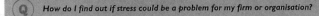

Q *How do I find out if stress could be a problem for my firm or organisation?*

A First, take informal soundings to get some idea of what problems there might be: for example, see if your staff are disillusioned with their work. This may show up as an increase in absenteeism (especially frequent short spells of sickness), lateness, disciplinary problems or staff turnover, or a reduction in output or quality of product or service. There may, of course, be other reasons for these symptoms, but if they could be related to stress at work, get your staff to tell you about it by:

- talking and listening to them. You could base the discussion on the sort of pressures mentioned in the middle of this booklet;
- asking them to describe the three 'best' and the three 'worst' aspects of their job, and whether any of these put them under uncomfortable pressure.

You can use the information you collect to identify common and persistent pressures, and who might be harmed by them.

Several off-the-shelf questionnaires do the same kind of thing. These can be helpful but tend to be lengthy and may not ask the type of questions that are relevant to your organisation. Also, interpreting the findings may require specialist knowledge.

Remember to:

- respect the confidentiality of your staff;
- tell your staff what you plan to do with any information you collect;
- involve them, as much as possible, in subsequent decisions;
- involve safety representatives, if you have them, in your plans and decisions;
- if you employ five or more staff, record the important findings from your risk assessment, for example by writing them down;
- check from time to time that the situation hasn't changed.

Q *If I do find out that stress is, or could be, a problem, what can I do about it?*

A There's no single best way of tackling work-related stress. What you do will depend on your working practices and the causes of the problem. But only providing training or help (or both) for sufferers won't be enough – it won't tackle the source of the problem! The boxes in the middle of this booklet show some of the pressures at work that might be relevant to smaller organisations, along with some suggestions about what to do.

3

WORK-RELATED STRESSORS

Culture

Problems that can lead to stress

- lack of communication and consultation
- a culture of blame when things go wrong, denial of potential problems
- an expectation that people will regularly work excessively long hours or take work home with them

What management can do

- provide opportunities for staff to contribute ideas, especially in planning and organising their own jobs
- introduce clear business objectives, good communication, and close employee involvement, particularly during periods of change
- be honest with yourself, set a good example, and listen to and respect others
- be approachable – create an atmosphere where people feel it is OK to talk to you about any problems they are having
- avoid encouraging people to work excessively long hours

Demands of the job

Problems that can lead to stress

- too much to do, too little time
- too little/too much training for the job
- boring or repetitive work, or too little to do
- the working environment

What management can do

- prioritise tasks, cut out unnecessary work, try to give warning of urgent or important jobs
- make sure individuals are matched to jobs, provide training for those who need more, increase the scope of jobs for those who are over-trained
- change the way jobs are done by moving people between jobs, giving individuals more responsibility, increasing the scope of the job, increasing the variety of tasks, giving a group of workers greater responsibility for effective performance of the group
- make sure other workplace hazards, such as noise, harmful substances and the threat of violence, are properly controlled

4

180

Control

Problems that can lead to stress

- lack of control over work activities

What management can do

- give more control to staff by enabling them to plan their own work, make decisions about how that work should be completed and how problems should be tackled

Relationships

Problems that can lead to stress

- poor relationships with others
- bullying, racial or sexual harassment

What management can do

- provide training in interpersonal skills
- set up effective systems to prevent bullying and harassment (ie, a policy, agreed grievance procedure and proper investigation of complaints)

Change

Problems that can lead to stress

- uncertainty about what is happening
- fears about job security

What management can do

- ensure good communication with staff
- provide effective support for staff throughout the process

Role

Problems that can lead to stress

- staff feeling that the job requires them to behave in conflicting ways at the same time
- confusion about how everyone fits in

What management can do

- talk to people regularly to make sure that everyone is clear about what their job requires them to do
- make sure that everyone has clearly defined objectives and responsibilities linked to business objectives, and training on how everyone fits in

Support and the individual

Problems that can lead to stress

- lack of support from managers and co-workers
- not being able to balance the demands of work and life outside work

What management can do

- support and encourage staff, even when things go wrong
- encourage a healthy work-life balance
- see if there is scope for flexible work schedules (eg flexible working hours, working from home)
- take into account that everyone is different, and try to allocate work so that everyone is working in the way that helps them work best

5

181

Remember to:

- involve your staff and their representatives – they are certain to have good ideas you could use;
- follow up any changes you make to ensure that they're having the effect you intended;
- review what you've done when you make major changes in your workplace (eg organisational change, new equipment, work systems or processes) to make sure that stress hasn't increased;
- lead by example – as a manager, you can communicate powerful signals about the importance of avoiding stress.

Q *But why would employees want to tell me about their stress?*

A You're right. Employees may be reluctant to admit they are feeling stressed by work. This is because being stressed can be seen as a sign of weakness. You can help by making it easier for your staff to discuss stress. Reassure them that the information they give you will be treated in confidence.

Q *What can I do to prevent stress from becoming a problem?*

A Most of the 'things to do' boil down to good management. They're ongoing processes that need to be built into the way your organisation is run.

- Show that you take stress seriously, and be understanding towards people who admit to being under too much pressure.
- Encourage managers to have an open and understanding attitude to what people say to them about the pressures of their work, and to look for signs of stress in their staff.
- Ensure that staff have the skills, training and resources they need, so that they know what to do, are confident that they can do it and receive credit for it.
- If possible, provide some scope for varying working conditions and flexibility, and for people to influence the way their jobs are done. This will increase their interest and sense of ownership.
- Ensure that people are treated fairly and consistently and that bullying and harassment aren't tolerated.
- Ensure good two-way communication, especially at times of change. Don't be afraid to listen.

Ask yourself whether you do these things. If you don't, or are unsure whether you do, take another look at the suggestions on 'what management can do' in the boxes in the middle of the booklet.

6

Q *What should I do if an employee complains about being stressed?*

A First, listen to them! If the stress is work-related:

- try to address the source(s);
- involve the employee in decisions;
- if necessary, encourage them to seek further help through their doctor;
- if you are not their line manager, ensure that he or she treats the employee with understanding and maintains confidentiality.

Where you can't control the work-related sources of stress, it may be appropriate to move the employee if you can. If a period of sick leave is recommended, keep in touch with the employee and their doctor. Remember that they may be able to return to work to do part of their job, work reduced hours or do a different job, before they are ready to return to their old one. Try to be flexible!

Don't be tempted to think that firing someone provides an easy way out! If you don't act reasonably in dismissing an employee, they could claim unfair dismissal.

Finally, bear in mind that if one of your employees is suffering from work-related stress, they may represent the tip of an iceberg. Find out whether others are also experiencing stress at work.

Q *Should I be providing stress management training?*

A Stress management training comes in various forms. It usually teaches people to cope better with the pressures they may come across. Because it focuses on the individual, it tends not to tackle the causes of stress at work. However, it can be useful as part of a 'bigger plan' to tackle work-related stress.

Q *Should I be providing a professional counselling service or an Employee Assistance Programme?*

A A counselling service is usually paid for by employers. It provides counsellors to whom individuals can talk privately about their problems. An Employee Assistance Programme (EAP) can provide various services (eg counselling, performance management, financial advice, legal assistance). You're not under any legal obligation to provide such services. Also, because these services must protect the confidentiality of the individual, the information they can give you may not help you tackle the causes of stress at work. On the other hand, like training, they can be useful as part of a 'bigger plan' to tackle work-related stress. So, consider carefully whether such services would fit your needs and provide value for money for your organisation.

7

Q Do I need external consultants to help me deal with this?

A In most cases, complex and expensive risk management procedures aren't necessary to tackle stress. Ordinary good management and regard for people may well be as effective as a high profile approach that might be recommended by outside consultants. But if you're worried that stress is a major problem and you can't deal with it internally, you could think about taking on an external consultant to help you. Make sure you choose them with care! Sources of help are listed below.

Q Where can I get more information or help?

A General advice is available from:

InfoLine, a confidential HSE phone service. Your calls will be charged at the national call rate. Tel: 08701 545500.

Your local HSE Inspector or the HSE Employment Medical Advisory Service (listed under 'Health and Safety Executive' in the phone book).

Your local authority inspector (listed under 'Local Authorities' in the phone book).

The Advisory, Conciliation and Arbitration Service (ACAS) can provide information and leaflets on employment rights and good management practices (listed under 'ACAS' in the phone book).

Chambers of Commerce can provide information and advice, consultancy services and training on a range of business-related issues, including health and safety. For details of your nearest Chamber, contact 020 7565 2000.

Employers' associations can sometimes provide advice on the problems that may lead to stress.

In March 2001, the Government launched a national campaign – *Mind Out for Mental Health* – to combat the stigma and discrimination surrounding mental health. *Working Minds* is the employer programme of the campaign. This part of the campaign works in partnership with employers to help improve workplace policy and practice on mental health. Visit www.mindout.net for more information.

8

A   **Advice on aspects of mental health is available from:**

The Health Development Agency, Trevelyan House,
30 Great Peter Street, London SW1P 2HW (Tel: 020 7222 5300).

The Health Education Board for Scotland, Woodburn House,
Canaan Lane, Edinburgh EH10 4SG (Tel: 0131 536 5500).

The National Assembly for Wales, Health Promotion Division – HP3, Cathays
Park, Cardiff CF10 3NQ (Tel: 02920 825111).

A   **Information on Employee Assistance Programmes is available from:**

EAPA (UK), Premier House, 85 High Street, Witney, Oxon, OX8 6LY
(Tel: 0800 783 7616).

A   **Advice on choosing external consultants is available from:**

The British Psychological Society, St Andrews House,
48 Princess Road East, Leicester LE1 7DR (Tel: 0116 254 9568).

A   **Also, you might like to refer to the following publications:**

*Tackling work-related stress: A managers' guide to improving and maintaining
employee health and well-being* HSG218 HSE Books 2001 ISBN 0 7176 2050 6

Managing work-related stress: A guide for managers and teachers in schools
HSE Books 1998 ISBN 0 7176 1292 9 provides good general advice that isn't
just relevant to those working in schools.

*Mental well-being in the workplace: A resource pack for management training and
development* HSE Books 1998 ISBN 0 7176 1524 3

Essentials of health and safety at work HSE Books 1994 ISBN 0 7176 0716 X

A   Our leaflets *Enforcement policy statement* (HSE Books 2002 HSC15) and *What
to expect when a health and safety inspector calls* (HSE Books 1998 HSC14), tell
you what to expect from us, and what you can do if you think we have not
treated you fairly.

While every effort has been made to ensure the accuracy of the references
listed in this publication, their future availability cannot be guaranteed.

9

HSE priced and free publications are available by mail order from HSE Books, PO Box 1999, Sudbury, Suffolk CO10 2WA Tel: 01787 881165 Fax: 01787 313995 Website: **www.hsebooks.co.uk** (HSE priced publications are also available from bookshops.)

For information about health and safety ring HSE's InfoLine Tel: 08701 545500 Fax: 02920 859260 e-mail: **hseinformationservices@natbrit.com** or write to HSE Information Services, Caerphilly Business Park, Caerphilly CF83 3GG. You can also visit HSE's website: **www.hse.gov.uk**

> This leaflet contains notes on good practice which are not compulsory but which you may find helpful in considering what you need to do.

This leaflet is available in priced packs of 10 from HSE Books, ISBN 0 7176 2112 X. Single free copies are also available from HSE Books.

INDG281rev1   **9/02**   **C1000**
Printed and published by the Health and Safety Executive

10

Useful websites

www.bullyonline.org – this is the website of the UK National Workplace Bullying Advice line. It provides practical advice to employers and employees on tackling bullying and provides summaries of recent case-law decisions.

www.cre.gov.uk – the Commission for Racial Equality works to encourage fair treatment in the workplace and to promote equal opportunities, regardless of race, colour or nationality.

www.disabilitymatters.com – Disability Matters Limited provides assessments of personal injury and income protection claimants who are prevented from working through disability. Its experts are able to advise on return to work requirements and its case managers co-ordinate services to facilitate return to work.

www.drc-gb.org – the Disability Rights Commission is an independent body, whose objective is to eliminate discrimination against disabled people and promote equality of opportunity. It provides advice and information for disabled people, employers and service providers. Contact it on 08457 622 633 for advice.

www.employers-forum.co.uk – the employers' forum is funded and managed by employers and is recognised as the authoritative voice on disability as it affects employers. The forum offers advice through a range of publications and events for employers.

www.eoc.org.uk – the Equal Opportunities Commission is the leading agency working to eliminate sex discrimination. It provides up-to-date information to help individuals and employers, publishes research and statistics on sex discrimination and takes on landmark legal cases under the Sex Discrimination Act and Equal Pay Act. Contact its helpline for further advice on 0845 601 5901.

europa.eu.int/eur-lex/en/index.html – part of the main European Commission site, this is the portal to an entire body of European law and includes all the pertinent EC/EU employment law directives.

www.harassment-law.co.uk – this website has been prepared by Barrister Neil Addison. It aims to provide practical information for anyone who is the victim of harassment or has been wrongly accused of harassment.

www.hse.gov.uk – the Health and Safety Executive is responsible for the regulation of almost all the risks to health and safety arising from work activity in Britain. Contact its 'Infoline' for further advice on 08701 545500.

www.legislation.hmso.gov.uk – this site includes UK Acts and Regulations dating from 1988.

www.nacab.org.uk – The National Association of Citizens' Advice Bureaux offers free, impartial and independent advice on a range of issues, including employment.

www.workplacebullying.co.uk – this site provides a legal resource for those working against bullying and harassment in the workplace. It contains summaries of recent case-law decisions, articles and research, which are easily understandable to the layperson. It is run by a non-profit-making organisation.

Index